PRAISE FOR SID AND THE BOYS

"*Sid and the Boys* is not only a feel-good story about a mid-America high school basketball team. It is a timeless tale of how fierce loyalty, selflessness, and mutual respect led a group of teenage boys and their beloved mentor to break down barriers and inspire their town. Told with heart, a keen attention to detail, and an awareness of how this undersized team fit into the big picture of a slowly evolving America, *Sid and the Boys* will have you cheering for the College High Wildcats as they take on corporate interference, systemic racism, and basketball opponents from around the state."

Lon Kruger, Head Coach, University of Oklahoma Men's Basketball

"Few of us knew at the time the full meaning and impact of our circumstances. That's another reason this story is important, and why we all appreciate the author's willingness to get it out there. After getting to know Carl McCullough on this journey, I sincerely believe that he was meant to tell it."

Ernie Jackson, graduate of College High School,
University of Notre Dame, and Columbia Law School

"This is a story that represents student-athletes on the scholastic level who demonstrated my philosophy in life and that is to never ever believe in CAN'T. With great coaching and a keen desire to excel, they became champs not only on the court but in the Game of Life!"

Dick Vitale, ESPN

SID AND THE BOYS

SID AND THE BOYS

Playing Ball in the Face of Race and Big Business

CARL McCULLOUGH

MAN TO MAN
PRESS

Published by Man to Man Press, LLC
www.SidandtheBoys.com

ISBN (paperback): 978-1-7364170-0-3
ISBN (e-book): 978-1-7364170-1-0

Images 1 through 7, 9 through 11, 13, 15, and 30 are Courtesy of the Bartlesville Area History Museum. 12 and 17 are Courtesy of the *Bartlesville Examiner-Enterprise*. The rest require no citation.

Cover and interior design by Christy Collins, Constellation Book Services

Printed in the United States of America

Dedicated to the memory of
Jo Allyn Lowe
1914-1975

Who served the youth of Bartlesville for over forty years
and more importantly led the way in living together.

CAST OF CHARACTERS

TEAM ROSTER
1966-67 COLLEGE HIGH SCHOOL WILDCATS

Coach: Sid Burton

Assistant Coach: Don Calvert

Starters:

Reserves: (Sometimes called "Scrub and the Subs")

Starters	Reserves
Ernest (Moody) Guery	Jim (Beetle) Bailey
Ernie (Eagle) Jackson	Jack (Big Jack) Brown
Scott (Sport) Martin	Mike (Chief) Dershem
David (Petey) Peterson	Steve (Supe) Hale
Pat (Boody) Sears	Larry (Cowboy or Scrub) Houchin
Bob (Moose) Larson	Mike (Louie) Louis

SUPPORTING CAST

Jo Allyn Lowe, Executive Director, Bartlesville Boys Club

Kenneth S. (Boots) Adams, Chairman and CEO,
Phillips Petroleum Company

Burl Stidham, Athletic Director, Bartlesville,
Oklahoma Public Schools

Paul Geymann, Athletic Director, Bartlesville Public Schools
following Stidham

CONTENTS

PREFACE

It was a chilly autumn evening in Meridian, Mississippi, when I first heard about the 1966-67 College High School Wildcat basketball team from my parents in Bartlesville, Oklahoma. I was in Navy flight training at the time and they were casually filling me in on hometown news. It went something like "Phillips is messing around with school coaches again." It sounded harmless enough—I was familiar with Phillips Petroleum Company's interaction with the school system, having grown up with it, and a vast majority of the time it was productive. They were reporting, though, in the context of recent high school coaching moves that hadn't been universally popular, to say the least.

We didn't discuss it in any detail, and the thought of that team and its coach vanished into the night. I was less than a year into my new career, and learning to fly Navy jets was fully consuming. It wasn't until fifty-two years later, while looking at Facebook posts from my old high school friends, that I noticed a picture of the four surviving starters of that team visiting with their 88-year-old coach. He had been inducted into the Bartlesville Sports Hall of Fame, but had been unable to travel to accept the award. Instead, those players accepted the award for him, and met at his home to deliver it. Those four players, plus one of their close friends, traveled to Bartlesville and Norman, Oklahoma, from

Tulsa, Houston, and as far away as Washington, DC, to be together with the coach.

Thus began my quest to learn more of the story about the unique relationship among the people in the picture. I knew the coach and most of the others, if only by name. Most, including the coach, I hadn't seen for nearly sixty years. Their story was heartwarming and inspiring, but to tell it, I had to know more about it. I contacted the two people in the picture that I knew best, former player Pat Sears and his close friend Marty Lowe. Those two men have aided immeasurably in the events since then. The coach as well as the other players—David Peterson, Scott Martin, and Ernie Jackson—have also contributed well beyond my expectations.

I confess up front that the story didn't turn out as I had envisioned. I began by writing about the Bartlesville that I knew while growing up there. It was a vibrant and seemingly progressive city, called by its Chamber of Commerce "America's Ideal Family Center" in 1950. In 1962, it was named an "All American City." After graduating from high school there in 1962, l left permanently, but not without very special, lasting memories of the good fortune I had to grow up there. The school system prepared me for a life I could never have envisioned—a Navy career that I wouldn't trade for anything, followed by experience in the highest levels of government. Many of my contemporaries had similarly rewarding careers.

Not everyone who grew up in Bartlesville had the same experiences. It didn't take long, as I researched this book, to uncover an unsettling side of life in my hometown. Readers expecting an account of fond memories will find them, but they may also learn, as I have, of events that make them uncomfortable. Those events don't detract from the inspiration that this story provides; in fact, they add to it. Ultimately, I learned that the qualities imbued in us from parents, teachers, and coaches like Sid Burton can prevail in the end, and leave a magical and lasting indelible mark.

For the Reader

This is a book about high school basketball, but it's a story about far more than that. It tells how a talented but undersized team and its coach encountered blatant examples of corporate interference and institutional racism, yet remained united and focused with one goal—to win a state basketball championship. For readers to understand and appreciate what the coach and team experienced, a discussion of a key term is in order.

Exactly what is "systemic racism?" It's certainly a term more frequently used in 2020 than sixty years ago. Various sources present the term as interchangeable with "institutional racism," which makes sense for the purpose of this story.

Although the phrase reportedly wasn't coined until 1967, the concept was actively practiced and embraced in Bartlesville, Oklahoma, for many years before that. In defense of Bartlesville and its residents, this was not a unique situation—then or now. In fact, the situation was typical of much, if not most, of America. Sadly, despite measurable progress in some areas of American life, it remains a problem. So what is it?

Institutional racism, according to *Wikipedia*, "is a form of racism that is embedded as normal practice within society or an organization. It can lead to such issues as discrimination in criminal justice, employment, housing, health care, political power and education, among other issues."

Bartlesville is singled out for a number of reasons. The first, and obvious one, is because that's where this story took place. It played a huge role in the lives of people in the story. Second, it's valuable because it *was typical*. It serves as a splendid example of how systemic racism looks, how subtle it can be, yet how impactful it is. It also provides a clear look at how oblivious people can be to the environment around them. To look at it another way, it's probably not systemic if you see it or think about it. There's an invisible sense to it—one that makes its existence easy to deny. That's the dangerous part of it.

Racial issues weren't new to northeastern Oklahoma in the mid-twentieth century, although the general public was largely unaware of them. Tulsa experienced one of the most significant racial massacres in history when hundreds of Blacks were killed in the Greenwood neighborhood in 1921. J. Edgar Hoover kick-started his career as a crime fighter in Osage County later in the twenties, by pursuing the cases of Native Americans being killed serially over oil disputes. In Bartlesville, the public librarian was dismissed in 1950 over her involvement in racial equality efforts. Notably, none of these events were discussed in public schools.

Whether the Greenwood and Osage County events fit the narrow description of systemic or institutional racism is debatable. Hate crimes? Yes. Racial prejudice? Yes. Fomented by institutional involvement? Certainly.

Companies like Phillips and Cities Service clearly played a role in the community. The son of a former Cities Service executive recently replied to a question from me. "I never met a salaried Black employee from Cities Service. Not in Bartlesville, and not in New York. I don't think they were excluded because of race, but because they lacked specific skill sets needed to conduct the business of the company."

That was written in 2020 about life in the fifties and is an explicit example of systemic racism, both then and now.

Ernie Jackson, a three-sport star athlete at College High School in the mid-sixties (and an honor graduate from Notre Dame with a law degree from Columbia University), recalls similar comments from Phillips employees while he performed temporary summer jobs for the company. "How could you hire every one of those new people, and believe they're all more qualified than every single Black jobseeker?" he would ask. A typical answer was, "Well, we'll have to send them to training," leaving Ernie to wonder why Black people weren't considered as trainable as their white counterparts. Ernie knew then, as he does now, that hiring a single Black applicant would have had a powerful, positive impact on the Black community, both in morale and economic terms.

Most strikingly, these hiring practices persisted in a company whose amateur basketball team was one of its leading marketing platforms. It's no secret that nationally known Black basketball stars would likely have played for the Phillips 66ers had they been deemed "suitable for the office environment." Marty Lowe recalls a prominent college All-American who was denied consideration for employment because the Phillips culture was not yet ready to accept a Black employee. No wonder that Black youth attending 66ers home games with other Boys Club members, courtesy of the company, would frequently cheer for the visitors, simply because they had Black players. Alonzo Adair was one of those fans of visiting teams. He knows that Phillips gave him tickets, and they also donated large sums of money to support the Boys Club. While he's appreciative of that, he views the Phillips actions as attempts to appease the Black community. "Keep them happy, but keep them in their place." It was easy for a Black kid in Bartlesville to cheer against an all-white team representing an all-white company.

Alonzo was aware of the few Black employees at Phillips, although they weren't visible to outsiders, filling jobs like handing out towels in the locker rooms or mopping floors after hours. But Alonzo also knew simply that Phillips provided no salaried positions for African Americans, and that meant no job security or upward mobility. Like others seeking professional careers, Alonzo couldn't wait to leave Bartlesville.

A footnote on Alonzo's career: Two years after accepting a football scholarship at Coffeyville (KS) Junior College, Alonzo transferred to Eastern Illinois, where he also played football. Upon graduation, he taught school and coached for a year in Saginaw, Michigan. In 1975, he considered two factors leading to another move. First, Saginaw was bitterly cold in the winter. Second, he learned that Phillips had "opened up" and was now hiring Black professionals. He returned to Bartlesville hoping for an interview. Unable to find one, he turned to a friend—a very high-placed friend. By then, the Phillips Chairman and CEO was William F. (Bill) Martin, whose son Scott had been a high school football teammate of Alonzo's. Martin greeted Alonzo warmly in his top-floor office and offered to help. They met on a Friday afternoon, and by Monday Alonzo had four interviews scheduled. Phillips hired Alonzo and retained him for twelve years before transferring him to Houston, where he ultimately left to pursue other career opportunities.

PROLOGUE

November 20, 1966

Mr. Paul Geymann
Director of Athletics
Bartlesville, Oklahoma

Dear Mr. Geymann:

It is the general opinion of the undersigned players that Sid Burton should be given the sole responsibility of coaching the varsity basketball team without the help of outside individuals.

We as players feel that this is not an unjust desire. We feel that the team spirit and morale is in a very depressed state when the presence of outside help is felt.

The undersigned players realize that the help is intended for our benefit, but we feel that this is doing more harm in the way of morale and spirit let down than the good that comes from the learning of more technique.

We would sincerely appreciate your consideration of this request.

Yours truly,

Signed by:

Jim Bailey
E. J. Barnes
Jack Brown
Mike Dershem
Richard Edgar (mgr)
Ernest Guery
Steve Hale
Larry Houchin
Ernie Jackson

Bob Larson
Michael Louis
Pat McCullough
Craig Martindale
David Peterson
Jim Powell
Pat Sears

Copies: Mr. John Haley
Mr. Tom Turvey
Mr. Sid Burton

Introduction

The Wildcats of Bartlesville's College High School kicked off the varsity basketball season the third week in November amid mixed reviews on their prospects of success. Four starters from the previous season returned, and while they had won over half their games and impressed observers with their hustle, they were a conspicuously short group. Averaging just over 5'11", the four were expected to be joined by an excellent athlete, Craig Martindale, adding valuable size to the lineup at 6'3". But the hopes of the team, school, and town were dashed in the eighth football game of the season on October 28 when Craig was helped off the field with a broken leg. The reaction of boosters was summed up by one who lamented, "There goes the basketball season."

Coach Sid Burton was beginning his second full season as head varsity coach after serving several years as an assistant in both football and basketball. A man with a full plate, Sid was a dedicated teacher of American History, and he worked in the spring as head varsity baseball coach. He inherited the hoops job from the beloved longtime coach, Bailey Ricketts, who stepped down early in the 1964-65 season due to poor health. Sid knew he had a tough job ahead, but liked his chances of improving the team's record. His lineup would feature two exceptional all-around athletes, junior Scott Martin and senior Ernie Jackson, who both stood 5'11". Some teammates referred to Scott as "Sport" because of his remarkable ability in tennis, golf, basketball, and football. He was a nationally ranked junior tennis player, and had just completed the football season as the team's starting quarterback. Ernie Jackson was a football teammate of Scott's and was known statewide for his speed, but it was his leaping ability on the hardwood that earned him the starting center position and the affectionate nickname "Eagle." According to his teammates, the Eagle "could flat jump out of the gym!"

Expected to join Sport and Eagle as returning starters was a pair with the unlikely names of Moody and Boody. Otherwise known as Ernest Guery and Pat Sears, the 6'½" Moody and the 5'11" Boody brought years of youth basketball experience and more great jumping ability to the Wildcat team. Sears was somewhat like Sport and Eagle, in that he participated in year-round varsity sports. A long-jumper for the track team, he had played quarterback in the fall until an injury turned him into a full-time kicker. Moody Guery, on the other hand, was a consummate "gym rat." Basketball was his first and only love in sports, and he dedicated seven days per week to it for fifty-two weeks every year. Dribble and shoot, rebound and shoot, follow and shoot— Moody knew the secret to winning was making more baskets than the other team, and to do that required taking a lot of shots. Sid had no one who worked harder on his shooting than Moody Guery. It was once said that "Moody couldn't jump over a nickel if you spotted him a dime," but he certainly knew how to establish position on the court. According to his classmate Marty Lowe, "his soft-looking physique belied a cat-like quickness and his gentle demeanor disguised a killer instinct on the court. On both ends of the floor, if Moody got you on his big backside, then he owned you!"

Midway through the first week of practice the cast was far from complete, but in the basketball-crazy town of Bartlesville, there would be plenty of competition to round out the roster.

PART 1

A Small City with Big Business

CHAPTER 1

IN THE BEGINNING: HUSHED BUT UNDENIABLE SIGNS

In the days preceding its incorporation, Bartlesville was known as a "sundown town," a term given to thousands of communities to describe their racial views and policies. The name is derived from rules requiring people of color to leave the area by sundown. In Bartlesville, the rule was applied inconsistently, depending on whether an occupant was an African American or Native American (or a Negro or Indian as they were known at the time). Prior to statehood in 1907, the Bartlesville region was part of Indian Territory, and featured a large population of Osages, Cherokees, and Delawares. Its founder, Jake Bartles, had taken an Indian bride, marrying the daughter of Delaware chief Charles Journeycake. Prior to Bartles' arrival in the area, the original town grist mill was owned by Nelson Carr, the only known white settler at the time. Carr's wife was a quarter-blood Cherokee, enough to gain him access into her nation.

Two other early residents of the area were William Johnstone and George Keeler. Both worked for Bartles and married Delaware women before setting out on their own and establishing local businesses. So it was clear from the very early days, well before Keeler, Johnstone, and Michael Cudahy discovered oil on the banks of the Caney River, that association with Indians was more than "just okay"—it was openly accepted and frequently rewarded. People with Black skin, on the other hand, were not only unwelcome after dark—there is very little mention of their role in the establishment of Bartlesville. The notable exception is the area's first physician, Dr. George Tann, who practiced in the Bartles settlement for several years, treating people of all races and building a small hospital. (Dr. Tann was also the family physician of the Ingalls family in *Little House on the Prairie* when they lived in southeast Kansas.)

The first school building in the newly incorporated town was Garfield School, originally built as a two-room wooden structure, and used to educate white children of all grade levels. Among its earliest students was the teenaged J. Paul Getty, who attended the school for two years before leaving with his father for California. The original schoolhouse was replaced in 1905 by a brick building at Sixth and Cherokee—just six blocks south of the original settlement—and Getty would be named by *Forbes Magazine* in 1966 as the world's richest private citizen.

Garfield School was followed in 1907 by the establishment of Douglass School, the first Bartlesville school for the town's estimated seven or eight African American children. These students attended a variety of one-room schools until 1912, when a brick building was completed to house students in grades one through eight. At that time, and for many years that followed, the Bartlesville Black community was limited to a small part of the town. Douglass School, located several blocks west of the town's only railroad tracks, was the nucleus of the neighborhood. The homes, which were typically small and poorly built, were located for the most part within three to five blocks of the school.

As schools and businesses sprang up, Bartlesville prospered and grew, albeit modestly, during the ten years that followed statehood.

Oil was the main attraction, and some who discovered it, like Keeler and Johnstone, were immortalized. Principal city streets were named for them, but it was the arrival of another family that would alter the course of history—in Bartlesville and around the world.

CHAPTER 2

THE EMERGENCE
OF BIG BUSINESS

The biggest thing to ever happen to Bartlesville was Phillips Petroleum Company, which for generations has been its biggest employer and funded nearly everything in town. In a December 2001 article, a writer for the *Tacoma (Wash.) News Tribune* said, "I never quite understood why the town where I spent my high school years wasn't named Phillipsburg. Nearly everything else in town was named after the Phillips Petroleum company or its founder."

So to understand the town of Bartlesville, knowing something about Phillips Petroleum Company is a necessity.

Frank Phillips, one of eleven children to grow up on the family farm in rural southwest Iowa, always yearned for more in his life than plowing fields. Ambitious even as a child, Frank would finish his chores at home and then dig potatoes for neighboring farmers for ten cents a day. At age fourteen, Phillips persuaded a barber in nearby Creston, Iowa, to take him on as an apprentice. Ten years later, Phillips owned all three barber shops in Creston, including one that was located in the basement of a bank. The bank president, John Gibson, was so impressed by Frank's ingenuity and ambition that he allowed the young man to marry his daughter, and invited Frank to join him in the bond business. Frank began selling bonds in the Northeast US, and one day ran into an old childhood friend, C.B. Larabee, while traveling through St. Louis, Missouri.

The two men got to talking, and C.B. told Frank about his work as a missionary to the Osage Indians just west of Bartlesville, Oklahoma, and how the area was rich in oil. Frank went back home and told his father-in-law about what he had learned, and the two men traveled there to see if C.B.'s rumors were founded. It turned out that they were, and with Gibson's assistance, Frank and his younger brother, L.E. Phillips, established the Anchor Oil & Gas Company in 1905. Based in Bartlesville, the Phillips brothers drilled their first wildcat well, the Holland No. 1, and got lucky when they struck oil on June 23, 1905, in what was still Indian Territory. The brothers must have had beginner's luck, because their second and third wells were dry. Nearly broke, but determined to make the company a success, they used the last of their funding to drill another well, the Anna Anderson No. 1. On September 6, 1905, their faith paid off, as this well was a gusher which the brothers leveraged to raise $100,000 through the sale of stock.

Frank had always dreamed of being a big-time banker, and in late 1905, heady with the success of the Anna Anderson well, he and L.E. took $50,000 in capital and formed Citizens Bank and Trust in Bartlesville. They also bought their rival establishment, Bartlesville National Bank, and consolidated the two under that name, which later became the First National Bank of Bartlesville.

In 1916, Frank and L.E. were weary of the boom-bust instability of the oil business and planned to switch exclusively to banking. They intended to open a chain of banks throughout the Midwest, but then World War I broke out and their careful plans were dashed. However, during wartime oil became a precious commodity, and the price increased from forty cents per barrel to more than $1 per barrel almost overnight. The brothers decided to consolidate their holdings in a single company, which they called Phillips Petroleum Company. When it incorporated under Delaware law on June 13, 1917, Phillips Petroleum Company had $3 million in assets, twenty-seven employees, and leases throughout Oklahoma and Kansas. It didn't hurt that America became enamored with automobiles during the decade that followed.

Frank was a demanding but well-loved boss. His employees called him "Uncle Frank" and knew that if they did their jobs well, they would be rewarded. Phillips once said to employees, "Work hard and demonstrate loyalty, and I'm a great guy to work for. Do neither, and there is no one worse."

One of his employees also recalls him remarking in his later years, "I am egotistical. I exercise the 'privilege and prestige of the office.' I'm bombastic, hard to get along with, an easy touch, a farm boy at heart, and conveniently hard of hearing. I'm just a sentimental old man. I'm tough and I know it. I'm the boss, and don't let anybody try to question it."

Frank Phillips led the organization as its president until 1938. The company had earned record profits of $24.1 million the year before, and at sixty-five years old he was ready to pass the torch to the next generation. Frank named Kenneth S. "Boots" Adams to succeed him as president, but became the first chairman of the board and remained such until he retired in 1949 at the age of seventy-six. He died a year later, but his legend lives on even today in Bartlesville, Oklahoma.

Frank Phillips

CHAPTER 3

BASKING IN THE BOOM

"The Athens of Oklahoma and the Garden Spot of the Great Southwest." Those were the words immortalized by Bailey Ricketts in describing Bartlesville to his high school world history students. Ricketts, who was also the beloved coach of the school's varsity basketball team, was referred to as "Father" by one of his players in the fifties. The moniker stuck, and he became Father to everyone in the school. It didn't hurt that he could easily be mistaken for a typical parish priest. His tongue-in-cheek comparison to ancient Greece stemmed from a local landmark, known simply as "The Mound," which straddled the Osage/ Washington County line on the western edge of town. The barren hill, or "Acropolis" to Father Ricketts, rose a staggering 151 feet above the surrounding flat terrain, and was adorned with a massive circular storage tank, or the Oklahoma version of the Parthenon.

By the 1960s, there were actually far more prominent landmarks in Bartlesville than The Mound. With about 28,000 residents, Bartlesville differed from other prairie cities of similar size by its conspicuous skyline of oil company office buildings. Noteworthy among them was the H. C. Price Tower, the first and only skyscraper designed by the acclaimed architect, Frank Lloyd Wright. The nineteen-story, 221-foot structure was described by Wright as "the tree that escaped the forest," and was built in 1956 to accommodate both offices and apartments. Harold C. Price had developed a mechanical electric welding apparatus for pipelines that revolutionized the ease with which pipe joints could be bound together (referred to as a "tie-in"), thereby significantly speeding up construction and improving safety and quality. Price was just one of many entrepreneurs lured to Bartlesville by the oil boom. Similarly, a Russian immigrant, Armais Arutunoff, came to the city with his invention, the electric submersible pump, which would soon provide immense benefits to the oil industry. Arutunoff began his work in Bartlesville in 1928, and received support for his work from Phillips Petroleum Company. The pump proved successful in the nearby oil fields, and soon led to the creation of a new company, REDA Pump, whose letters stand for "Russian Electrical Dynamo of Arutunoff." (In later years, REDA would become part of TRW, Inc., and then Schlumberger.)

While the Price Tower stood out as an architectural marvel, it was hardly alone in the Bartlesville skyline. Like the rest of the town, the silhouette was dominated by Phillips Petroleum Company. Phillips, however, wasn't the first energy company to establish roots in Bartlesville. Through a New York-based holding firm, Cities Service Company, Bartlesville became the base for the Empire Gas and Fuel Company in 1914. A nine-story building, Bartlesville's tallest at the time, eventually became known as the Cities Service Building. (Later known as the Cities Service Oil Company, it moved its headquarters to Tulsa in 1964, was purchased by Occidental Petroleum Company in 1982, and marketed its products under the name CITGO. Its headquarters are now in Houston, Texas.)

Phillips added substantially to the Bartlesville skyline by completing the Frank Phillips Tower in 1930, a building that provided office space for the rapidly growing company. It sufficed as the central headquarters location for another twenty years, until Phillips completed a state of the art, twelve-story high-rise called the Adams Building. The building's namesake, Boots Adams, was the protégé of Frank Phillips from the early days of the company, and became a prominent figure in the story that follows. The Adams Building, completed in 1950, contained eleven floors of offices, as well as an eight-lane bowling alley, cafeteria, Olympic-sized swimming pool, men's club, and a multi-purpose gymnasium that could seat 2,600 fans for basketball games or convert its surface for roller skating. It also featured modern tunnels connecting the building to the older Frank Phillips Tower and to an employee parking lot across the railroad tracks a block west of the Phillips office complex. Those tunnels doubled as shelters from the frequent storms that threatened "Tornado Alley" when dozens of families responded to blaring sirens.

Another high-rise building was completed directly across the street from the Adams Building in 1964, and Phillips broke ground twenty years later for yet another office building, this one fifteen stories tall. By the mid-eighties, approximately one-fourth of the company's 7,400 employees were based in Bartlesville.

As Phillips grew, the town of Bartlesville followed. What began as a tiny settlement along the banks of the Caney River evolved by mid-century into a desirable place to raise a family—at least for a vast majority of the residents. By 1950 the original business district had expanded south and west from the Caney to encompass a twenty-square block area, bounded roughly by Cherokee Street on the east to Jennings on the west, and between 1st and 5th Streets on the north and south edges. There were numerous prominent buildings beyond that perimeter—notably a hospital and the Washington County Courthouse a block east of Cherokee, the public library just south of 6th Street, and several businesses lining 3rd Street, or U.S. Highway 60, as it stretched west from downtown toward the airport in neighboring Osage County. One large church, First Baptist, lay within the perimeter, and several others snuggled up to downtown on its south side. Among them were First Presbyterian, First Methodist, First Christian, and St. John Catholic Church, all with large congregations, and also within walking distance to the business district.

Many Bartians, as the residents were known, could be identified by the church they attended—even more by their elementary school neighborhood. Kids in the far southwest corner of town attended Jane Phillips, named for Frank's wife. East of them were McKinley families, and between McKinley and downtown was the Horace Mann neighborhood. In a town where presidents' names were frequently used to name schools, Garfield and Jefferson were located just south and east of downtown, and Washington and Lincoln were on the west side. The only other schools west of the Caney River were St. John, a Catholic parochial school, and Douglass for Bartlesville's small Black population. Until the mid-1950s, when new homes brought new schools, the only elementary schools east of the Caney were Highland Park and Limestone. Central Junior High and College High School were south of downtown, just a few blocks from the west bank of the Caney.

Some of the neighborhoods had distinguishing characteristics. Many of the older homes were found near the town's origins—near Garfield and Jefferson schools, and on streets named for Indian tribes, like Osage, Cherokee, Shawnee, Wyandotte, and Delaware. Most homes were modest, but there was a sprinkling—largely along South Cherokee—that were mansion-like and were owned by the town's wealthiest families. As the neighborhood extended a mile south from Central Junior High to College High School, there were newer homes, built for wealthier or more established families, and featuring three or more bedrooms and multiple baths. At 14th Street, Cherokee Avenue became Hillcrest Drive, and two blocks further south, at the northern edge of the College High campus, lived the Martin family—Bill, Betty, Sherry, and Scott.

Until eastward expansion in the mid-fifties led to larger homes built across the Caney River, the newer homes were the postwar houses in the Jane Phillips area. New as they were, they were typically small—two bedroom, one bath, one-car garage homes built for young families just moving to Bartlesville. Yet, they were well built and comfortable, and served as an ideal place to raise children.

Phillips Mansion

Less than a mile north of Jane Phillips lay the westside neighborhood where Black Wildcat basketball prospects Ernie Jackson, Ernest Guery, and Mike Louis grew up. While the area wasn't crowded, many of the homes definitely were. Ernie's family with its twelve children wasn't typical, but the cramped conditions in his home were shared by many families. There was no air conditioning (although that was common in many other neighborhoods) and, in many cases, no indoor plumbing. Homes were old and often of flimsy construction. Kids found relief in the hot summers by running water from wells and dousing each other in playful games.

The downtown area was filled with prosperous businesses. Within the twenty-square-block area were three movie theaters, department and hardware stores, car dealerships, banks, upscale clothing shops, music and jewelry stores, and a newspaper office, all in addition to the sizable Phillips and Cities Service office buildings. Parking meters, first used in Oklahoma City in 1935, came to Bartlesville soon afterward and were fixtures throughout the business district.

Bartians were proud of their town, including their churches and schools. Their heritage included local legends like the Phillips brothers, Boots Adams, William Keeler, Paul Endacott, Armais Arutunoff, and H. C. Price, all key to the growth of Bartlesville from its pre-oil days to the bustling town it had become in the mid-sixties. But there were others, notably all men, who were pioneers in other ways. Bartlesville natives take justifiable pride in the town's many "firsts."

- The first troop established by the Boy Scouts of America was in nearby Pawhuska in 1909, and was soon followed by Troop 1 in Bartlesville's First Christian Church.

- George Getty was an attorney in the bonds and insurance industry who moved to Bartlesville in 1903. Before his interest turned to oil, Getty helped his son, J. Paul, launch his business career selling magazines on the streets of Bartlesville. The younger Getty was listed first in the world by the *Guinness Book of Records* in its 1966 list of richest private citizens in the world.

- Famed aviator Wiley Post, with financial backing from Frank Phillips, took off from the Bartlesville airport and made the first ever flight to the edge of the stratosphere on December 7, 1934.

- Oklahoma's first Little League baseball program was established in Bartlesville in 1953.

- Pay-for-view television made its national debut there in 1957 with a showing of *The Pajama Game* starring Doris Day and John Raitt.

- Marlex, the plastic product used to make Hula Hoops— and much more—was invented by Phillips chemists in the fifties.

Lesser known, but no less influential to many, were two other Bartians, Jo Allyn Lowe and Sid Burton. Lowe, with assistance from H.C. Price and other community leaders, established Oklahoma's first Boys Club in Bartlesville in 1954. Burton, a product of Bartlesville schools, was also offered assistance from Phillips. History shows it was unnecessary, and Burton delivered another memorable first to the community as the high school's beloved basketball coach.

The Mound

Price Tower

Skyline

CHAPTER 4

THE MARTINS' TOWN

William F. (Bill) Martin embodied the story of Bartlesville. It was a town built around oil and made famous by its basketball program. In 1966, Bill was the heir apparent to men who built Phillips Petroleum Company and its powerhouse amateur basketball team. Frank Phillips had established the company, and one of his early hires was Kenneth S. (Boots) Adams, a former University of Kansas basketball player. Adams, in turn, established a basketball team, named them the Phillips 66ers, and hired another Kansas player, Paul Endacott, to join the company as an engineer in 1923, but soon persuaded him to join the basketball team. Endacott enjoyed an exceptional college career, leading Kansas to national championships in 1922 and 1923, and being named the Helms Foundation National Player of the year as a senior. The legendary Kansas coach Phog Allen called the 5'10" Endacott the best player he ever coached. He was an active member of the 66ers' roster from 1924 -1928.

From the twenties through the fifties, one thing about working at Phillips was clear: success on the basketball court led to success on the corporate ladder. Just as Adams replaced Frank Phillips as company president, Endacott followed Adams. In 1966, Adams still ran Phillips as its board chairman, and Endacott was serving in his fifteenth year as company president.

Unlike Adams and Endacott, Bill Martin was a University of Oklahoma graduate, albeit one with similar athletic credentials. In his Sooner career, spanning 1935-38, Bill won conference tennis championships in both singles and doubles, and was named to the all-conference basketball team as a 6'1" guard and forward. His senior team at OU became known as the "Boy Scats" because of their upbeat tempo and the leadership of another future 66er, Jimmy "Scat" McNatt. An excellent student as well, Bill earned the university's prestigious Letzeiser Award for scholastic achievement and citizenship.

Martin joined Phillips in 1939 as a clerk in the treasury department and quickly earned a spot on the basketball team. Despite taking three years away for service in the Army, he was named an AAU All-American three times in the forties. He and Betty Jean Randall, both from Blackwell, Oklahoma, were married in 1941 and welcomed a daughter Sherry in 1945. Their only other child, Scott, was born in 1950, and by the time Scott reached high school, Bill was senior vice president of Phillips.

Scott remembers growing up in Bartlesville as an exceptional opportunity. His teachers at Garfield Elementary School were talented and dedicated, and though many years removed from the days of J. Paul Getty, they remained focused on providing students with the tools for success in life. Scott was no exception. His after-school life centered on athletics, and he plunged wholeheartedly into whatever sport was in season. His home, in one of the town's more elite neighborhoods, was directly across from College High School, with only the school's tennis courts between the Martin house and the football stadium.

"I was gifted by God with above average athletic ability and started playing sports at a young age. I was best at tennis but always liked basketball the most."
Scott Martin, 2020

Scott picked up tennis skills from his dad, and by the time he was ten, he was regularly playing in state, regional, and national tournaments. The Martin family also belonged to the prestigious Hillcrest Country Club, with its scenic, up-and-down golf course located on the south edge of town, and that was where Scott developed into a low-handicap golfer before his teenage years. Hillcrest catered to Bartlesville's upper income families, and its all-white membership included doctors, attorneys, bankers, merchants, and high-level managers and executives of the town's leading companies. A second whites-only country club, Sunset, located on the far northwest side of town, provided a less expensive golf experience, as did Adams Municipal Course on the eastern edge of town.

Scott enjoyed the same benefits as other Phillips dependents, although he seldom had time to use all of them. He and his future high school teammates (those whose fathers worked for Phillips) acquired their basketball skills on that court, often under the tutelage of current and former 66ers like Denny Price and Charlie Bowerman, both AAU All-Americans in the early sixties. The coaches stressed fundamentals like passing and dribbling with either hand, keeping eyes up, making free throws. Their ball-handling skills developed into material for 66er halftime shows, with routines mimicking the Harlem Globetrotters. These youngsters, dubbed the Phillips 33ers, learned at an early age how to perform in primetime in front of large crowds.

Frank Phillips ensured that outdoor recreation would also be available for his employees and their families and friends. In 1925 he established a 3,700-acre ranch and wildlife preserve as his personal retreat. Just twelve miles southwest of downtown Bartlesville in the Osage Hills, it soon became a gathering place for Frank's "outlaw and Indian" friends' parties, and later for company picnics. Frank added a museum to the property, one that houses an extraordinary collection of western and Native American art and memorabilia.

According to Gerald Thompson, College High School Class of 1970, "There were a lot of places in Bartlesville where we Black people couldn't go. We didn't know about many of the places you're mentioning. Our parents protected us from the ugliness they faced when they left the neighborhood."

Bill Martin kept Scott busy with sports, but never at the expense of his school work. For his all-around athletic prowess, Scott became known to his friends as "Sport," but his teachers knew him as a straight-A student. Bill was a master with numbers—especially money—and was known throughout the oil industry for his financial management skill. It seemed inevitable that Scott would follow in his father's footsteps—an exceptional athlete and stellar student. Somehow, he even found time to play in a band, although he's quick to say now that they "weren't very good."

Life in Bartlesville, however, *was* very good for the Martin family—and Scott hadn't yet made his biggest splash as a high school athlete.

Another opinion: "The Acemen (Scott Martin, BJ Steinbrook, Tommy Blachly, Gene Holt, and Tom Murry) were the most popular band in town from the College High class of '68. BTW, Tom Murry became CEO of Calvin Klein—that Calvin Klein."

Marty Lowe, 2020

CHAPTER 5

THROUGH EAGLE'S EYES

"Black Jack" and Bettye Jackson raised their family across town from the Martins—*way* across town. In a neighborhood of mostly small, poorly maintained homes, Bartlesville's Black population sat anchored within a few city blocks of Douglass Elementary School. Geographically, the Martin and Jackson homes were only a couple of miles apart. Culturally, they were much further.

Another Bettye, this one named Williams, recalls moving to Bartlesville in 1955, just after her husband Sheldon completed training in dry cleaning at Oklahoma State Technical College in Okmulgee. He was offered a job at Rowe Cleaners and jumped at the opportunity to live in Bartlesville. Upon arrival, they found a very limited area in which to seek housing; Bettye recalls that it had to be west of Santa Fe and north of 9th Street. Black families were confined to a small area, not only because they weren't welcome in other neighborhoods, but also because Douglass was, until 1955, the only school that would admit Black children. To their surprise and dismay, the Williams couple found only one home available, a rental that lacked any indoor water supply. Bartlesville, the "progressive" town they had heard about, was nothing like Okmulgee. It was difficult to make ends meet in a town where wages for Black workers were comparatively miniscule.

Ernie described his house like this: *"It was a one-story wood frame house with dark green siding and a screened-in porch stretching the width of the structure. It had seven rooms with a short hallway leading to the back of the house onto a utility room with a washing machine that had one of the old-fashioned clothes wringers that you fed clothes through manually. There was a separate living room, dining room, and kitchen; three bedrooms; no formal bathroom (until one was installed my third grade year with indoor plumbing). We had an outhouse in the early years, as well as what would be the equivalent of a chamber pot for use at night. We used large tin tubs for bathing, sometimes three kids at a time in one tub. In the absence of indoor running water, our drinking water was contained in a large metal pail with a dipper. The kitchen had an 'ice box' rather than a refrigerator. The upper portion held blocks of ice that kept the interior cool. The ice was replaced/replenished every four or five days, as I recall.*

The house was a little drafty, and I recall that for a while we used a wood burning stove to heat the house for at least one winter. Of course it was mostly effective if you sat close to it. That wasn't always possible because the sides would get glowing, red hot and presented the risk of someone getting burned. There was no air conditioning (until the new house was built during my freshman or sophomore year) so we used electric fans during the summer.

Since many of my older siblings had left home by that time, there were about six or seven of us children who lived in the house with our parents."

Westside Community

> *"The median nonwhite family income—a median skewed by the wealth of oil-rich Indians—was about a third that of the median family income."*
> Louise S. Robbins

Across the tracks from their own homes, Black people found jobs caring for white families' children, cleaning their homes, and mowing their lawns. They could also walk four miles to Hillcrest Country Club to carry the golf bags of the town's wealthier residents. Although they weren't allowed inside the clubhouse/pro shop, they were more than welcome to work as caddies. Everett Adair recalls his days caddying at Hillcrest in the early sixties. He was a small kid—too small to carry bags like his older, bigger friends—so he pushed and pulled the golf bags on a cart. Up and down the hilly course he walked, most days with temperatures in the nineties, earning about $2.50 for eighteen holes. He quit after about three years, knowing how easy it was to blow his earnings on one sandwich at the club. Ev spent his remaining school years helping his father mow lawns around town.

One of the community's unsung heroes was a friend of Bettye Williams and the Jackson family, Mazie Wooten, who spent years caring for young Black children while their mothers worked as domestic helpers for the white families. Miss Mazie, as everyone called

Westside Homes

her, had children of her own, including sons Larry and Ernest Guery, both of whom showed basketball skill at an early age. As Mom was working, the boys disappeared down the street to the Boys Club, where they played countless hours on the only court in town that was open to them—outside of the schools. Marty Lowe remembers how Miss Mazie was designated as the unofficial "historian" of the local Black community—the one who, until her death in 1986, was the "go-to" person when it came to running down Boys Club alumni who had left the area. She treated all the kids as her own, and never lost track of them. Marty described her as "a loving, caring person who was beloved by her community with good reason."

After Bettye Williams' first home was destroyed by fire and the family once again struggled to find suitable housing, things began to change in Bartlesville and around the country. Central Junior High (grades seven through nine), and College High School both opened their doors to Black students following the U.S. Supreme Court's landmark *Brown v. Board of Education* decision, and Douglass was reduced to grades one through eight. Elementary schools were legally integrated, but remained segregated by neighborhoods. Only the few Black children on West 9th Street, east of the railroad tracks, could attend schools other than Douglass.

"My mother worked as a maid throughout her working life, cleaning houses and hotel rooms early on. My father owned and operated what was then called a 'joint,' the equivalent of a honky-tonk or bar, and modeled on the black Southern establishments of the time. It was a place where you could buy bootleg and legal alcohol. Its primary activities involved dominoes, card games, and dice. In short, it was a place where poor and working class Blacks, whites, and Native Americans went to socialize and relax."

Ernie Jackson, 2020

One of those was Jane Morrison, a high school senior. She and her family were among the first Blacks on that short dead-end street. When schools in Bartlesville and nationwide were desegregated in 1955, Jane was forced to attend the newly integrated College High School—after attending Douglass the previous eleven years. That process had its predictable hiccups, but none was more significant than prom night—when Jane couldn't attend because no white boy invited her, and her Black boyfriend, Wayne Chambers, wasn't allowed to attend because he wasn't a College High student. Jane sought a waiver from the principal, which was denied, so she stayed home on prom night.

That was the Bartlesville that Ernie Jackson knew when he turned six, but as desegregation began, Ernie's parents had other plans. Black Jack and Bettye had nine other children before Ernie and his twin

Douglass School

brother Bernie were born in 1949. In order of birth, they were Leon, Delitha, Donald, Junetta, Charles, Mary Lou, Sarah (Sunny), and twins Gloria Jean and Marcelline. Ernie's twin brother died in infancy, but the parents soon added Shirley and Rickie to the fold. Bettye, a devout Catholic, enrolled the younger half, including Ernie, in Bartlesville's only parochial school, St. John Catholic. Ernie recalls being the school's only Black male student, but benefiting from "a very good education, comfortable social environment, and good classmates and friends."

Much like Scott Martin, Ernie enjoyed sports throughout the year. St. John had fewer teams, but Ernie found competition in sandlot and Little League baseball, neighborhood football, and Boys Club basketball. There, at a place they simply called "the club," he met guys like Pat Sears, Scott Martin, Bob Larson, and David Peterson. Along with Marty Lowe, Larry Houchin, and Ernest Guery, Ernie and his friends grew to appreciate each other for their diversity and skill. Ernie was universally admired—by his friends, schoolmates, teachers, and other adults. He learned respect and responsibility from his parents and older siblings, and found it easy to get along with everyone. He served as an altar boy at St. John, and other than sneaking an occasional sip of wine behind the priest's back, he was generally well behaved. Bettye Williams recalls how she could always rely on Ernie for help, particularly in her community service activities. The Black community had an extraordinary sense of togetherness, epitomized by families like the Williams and Jacksons.

"*My best friend at St. John was Steve B., who was a rebellious free spirit with a good heart. His mother worked behind the soda counter at H.L. Green five and dime store downtown, only a few blocks from the school. On days when school let out early, Steve would sometimes go to H. L. Green's for an afternoon meal served by his mom. Once he invited me to go with him to see her. I went, thinking we'd only be there a short time and then be on our way to other adventures. She enthusiastically greeted us when we arrived and told us to sit at the counter so she could serve us a meal. I certainly wasn't expecting that and was more than a little shocked, since the counter was off limits for Blacks. I thought to myself, 'uh, oh; I can't do that,' and politely told her so. Her response was, 'Boy, you better come on over here and sit down like I told you to!' And I did. As expected, some of the other customers, mostly adults, would glance over and stare at us in surprise, confusion, and apparent disapproval. It was then that I realized from where Steve got his good-hearted rebellious nature.*"

Ernie Jackson, 2020

CHAPTER 6

PETEY AND THE PAPERBOYS

Bartlesville in the fifties and sixties was a town known to many by its neighborhood schools. To others, nearly all of them boys, it was also known by its paper routes. David Peterson, called "Petey" by his friends, grew up on the town's far southwest side, where he attended Jane Phillips Elementary School and Central Junior High School. Then, prior to starting his eighth grade year, his family moved to the Rolling Hills neighborhood on Bartlesville's east side. Beginning as a ninth grader at Madison Junior High School and continuing through his senior year, Petey delivered the *Bartlesville Examiner-Enterprise* on weekday evenings and Sunday mornings. Petey recalls having a "one hundred percent route," meaning that every one of the two hundred homes in his neighborhood subscribed to his paper. He credits pedaling his bicycle over the hilly route for developing strong legs which helped him achieve success in both basketball and tennis. Even hillier than Petey's route was the one Pat Sears traversed in Pennington Hills. Pat, or "Boody" as he was known, lived near Will Rogers Elementary School, and had a long stretch of three hilly streets—Greystone, Wilshire, and Elmhurst—to deliver the morning editions of the *Tulsa World*. Even though Boody was only a substitute paper boy, he also developed calf muscles that he credits for making him an exceptional jumper.

> *"The paper was just the right size so that I could ride my bicycle down a street and throw each paper onto the porch of every house on the route. If I missed the porch, I would get off of my bike and put the paper on the porch. I would return to my house once or twice each day to reload with newspapers."*
>
> David Peterson, 2020

Those routes, as well as others, were known by their clientele. A classmate of Petey and Boody, Pat McCullough delivered papers to the door of H.E. Kirchner, a 6'10" center for the Phillips 66ers. Kirchner was a hulk of a man—a graduate of Texas Christian University who seemed to be as wide as he was tall. Pat and his brother Mike frequently wondered how Kirchner could get in and out of the step-down front door of his small eastside apartment. Just to bend down for the paper seemed like a mammoth effort for a gentle giant. Jim Hess, who was a few years older than Boody and Petey, recalled how another 66er, the 6'5" Bill Hoagland, would sit on his front steps and chat with Jim as he circled the neighborhood near Garfield School delivering the evening papers.

Other Bartlesville youngsters figured out less strenuous ways to sell their papers. Jon Harkavy and the Pierce brothers, Jay and Jerry, were non-Phillips kids (unlike Peterson, Sears, and the McCulloughs) who met the paper distributor near Phillips headquarters, and sold their stacks of papers to employees as they left the Adams and Phillips Buildings in the late afternoon.

There were also the June boys, Mike and Jim, whose father, K.I., became the city's postmaster. They took early advantage of Bartlesville's eastward expansion, establishing paper routes for the *Tulsa World* as Pennington Hills added neighborhoods with hundreds of new homes. Those homes brought new customers, and K.I. June taught his boys entrepreneurship that paid off handsomely. Mike and Jim earned spending money, jackets, trips, and college assistance for their many years of delivering morning papers.

Out on the route

David Peterson was the second of four children of Bruce and Velma. Along with his older sister, Marilyn, and younger siblings, Dennis and Barbara, he grew up in a modest home near the southwest edge of Bartlesville. His neighborhood was built in the late nineteen forties to accommodate the surge in postwar hiring by Phillips Petroleum Company, and the nearby grade school, Jane Phillips, was named for the wife of the company's founder. The school, like others citywide, had an extraordinary principal and teachers, making the school system one of the country's finest. Phillips and another major oil company, Cities Service, contributed to the town's ranking as one of the nation's tops in per capita income and PhDs. Throughout Petey's childhood, his hometown was recognized as one of the finest places in America to live. Called "America's ideal family center" by the Chamber of Commerce in 1950, it was named an "All-American City" in 1962. Petey's life exemplified the opportunities of growing up there. He was active in the First Methodist Church, Boy Scouts, Little League, and sports sponsored by Phillips and the local Boys Club. In Scouts, he attained the rank of Eagle and traveled to the 1964 National Jamboree in Valley Forge, Pennsylvania. He loved baseball, particularly northeast Oklahoma's favorite player, Mickey Mantle, a native of Commerce. Once, when the Yankees visited Kansas City, David and his father boarded a train to go see the "Commerce Comet" play centerfield. Every kid in town loved Mickey, but the favorite major league team by far was the St. Louis Cardinals. Their beloved broadcaster, Harry Caray, dominated the airwaves for years with his play-by-play descriptions of Stan Musial, Lou Brock, and Bob Gibson. Caray's broadcasts were heard on dozens of stations throughout Arkansas, Missouri, Kansas, and Oklahoma, and provided nightly entertainment during Bartlesville summers.

Petey and his close friend, Craig Martindale, shared in a host of sporting activities. Their basketball careers began in the Peterson driveway, and the family's large corner lot hosted countless games of baseball and football. Together, along with Boody Sears, they played on the Tie-Ins Little League baseball team. Petey and Craig attended Jane Phillips together, and as sixth graders won the city's grade school basketball tournament. About that time, Petey's basketball activities expanded to include teams at the local Boys Club and in the Phillips gymnasium. He, Martindale, Boody Sears, and a young Scott Martin developed their skills with the Phillips 33ers, a fun-loving group led by some of the seasoned Phillips 66ers. Some of the same kids ventured about three quarters of a mile west, a couple of blocks beyond an expansive Phillips parking lot, to the Bartlesville Boys Club. There they were able to play with some of Bartlesville's Black youth, including Ernie Jackson and Ernest Guery, two extremely likable boys who quickly became their friends. Martin, Peterson, Jackson, and Guery became part of a stellar fourteen-and-under team that won the Oklahoma State AAU championship, with help from Central Junior High classmates like Bob Larson and Larry Houchin. Boody Sears, normally a fixture in that group, turned fifteen on December 28, 1963, and was three days too old for their age group.

Boys Club 14 and Under AAU Champs

CHAPTER 7

BOODY'S BURBS

Gerald Orlando (G.O.) Sears, Jr., and his wife Neva moved to Bartlesville in 1951 with their sons Mike and Pat. G.O. was a new Phillips employee, attracted to his new home by a bustling economy and the promise of good schools for his sons. He and Neva added a baby girl, Janet, in 1955, soon after Pat acquired the nickname Boody. Why Boody? As Pat tells it, he was led by Mike and his parents to become a fan of the Cleveland Indians baseball team. The Indians featured a star shortstop, a future Hall-of-Famer named Lou Boudreau. Why Mike called his little brother "Boudreau" is anybody's guess, but it was gradually shortened to "Boody." The rest, as they say, is history. Boody and Mike entered the brand new Will Rogers Elementary School in 1955, Pat as a first grader, and Mike three years ahead. The school was built on the bank of a small creek that crossed Frank Phillips Boulevard, three miles east of downtown Bartlesville. The Sears home had been completed the previous year, and was part of a major expansion to parts east of the Caney River. Bartlesville had grown up around the intersection of two major interstate highways, U.S. 75 running north to south from Kittson County, Minnesota, to Dallas, Texas, and U.S. 60, running east to west from Virginia Beach to Los Angeles. The town's eastern suburbs had been served for years by two elementary schools along Highway 75, Highland Park to the northeast and Limestone to the southeast. By the mid-fifties, the growth of Phillips had spawned other expansion, and multiple oil-related companies blossomed. Companies like Cities Service, REDA Pump, National Zinc, and H. C. Price provided jobs for hundreds of Bartlesville residents. Price, the founder of a large pipeline enterprise, hired famed architect Frank Lloyd Wright to design a building for him—one that would accommodate offices and apartments. Completed in 1956, the nineteen-story Price Tower became nationally recognized as Wright's only skyscraper.

> *"I can't really think of a singular person that was an influence on my playing any sports. I am certain I just followed my brother in whatever he was playing at the time. My brother was excellent in organizing neighborhood kids in football, basketball, and baseball. My dad never had to ask either of us to go outside and play sports. It was just what life was supposed to be."*
>
> Pat Sears, 2020

Amidst this expansion a new neighborhood was created. Its developers called it Pennington Hills, and its new schools included Will Rogers Elementary in 1955, and Hoover Elementary and Madison Junior High in 1958. All of them opened their doors to children of all races, but there were no Black families living on Bartlesville's east side as long as Boody was in school there.

Boody's life on the east side mirrored Petey's in southwest Bartlesville, but Boody was more of a free spirit, priding himself in the mischief he created and sometimes leading others astray. He was a favorite of Jo Allyn Lowe's in pulling pranks, and his tendencies for fun and games got him into hot water with Sid Burton more than once during his junior year. The Peterson, Sears, and Lowe families were all members of the First Methodist Church, and although Boody sometimes attended, he was more likely to steal away to the Rexall Drug Store than partake in Bible studies.

"The idea of rebellion against the establishment probably occurred when I was student body president at Madison Junior High. Many of my friends were more than disgusted with the cafeteria food choices. Monty (Johnson) and I organized a sack lunch day on the hush hush. The word spread and we probably had a hundred kids that were gonna bring their sack lunches. The word got around so well that a teacher found out and told the principal. In his best judgement as to how to resolve the issue, the principal, Mr. Littlefield, invited me to his office. Without him knowing who was responsible for the sack lunch day, he wanted me to address the student body over the intercom during second-hour announcements, to cease with the arrangement. I was never so embarrassed. After that fiasco, I decided politics and the compromising issues you find yourself in were not for me."

Pat Sears, 2020

G.O. Sears and Bruce Peterson both worked for Phillips so all their children experienced the company's benefits. Both boys had paper routes, although Petey's was an every-day route carrying the evening Bartlesville paper while Boody only occasionally delivered Tulsa's morning edition. They were teammates on the Tie-Ins Little League team, and played together at both the Boys Club and Phillips gyms.

They opposed each other as seventh graders, with Petey playing for Central and Boody for Madison, but a Peterson family move to Pennington Hills in 1963 brought them together for their eighth grade season. The following year, Ernie Jackson left St. John Catholic School for Central Junior High, where he joined Ernest (Moody) Guery from Douglass and Scott (Sport) Martin from Garfield to form a team that Boody and Petey couldn't beat—ever.

> *"There were plenty of other colorful moments—some not suitable for print. Among them were when Marty, Moose, Moody, and I were named the 'equine custodians' in the parade honoring Boots' Adams 66th birthday, and had to follow the horses, cleaning up after them in a driving rainstorm—all decked out in our best Boys Club paisley outfits. Or joyriding with three of us packed into my '59 Fiat, or forming a 'sewer brigade'—a mission to check out the city's underground system. The list goes on…"*
>
> Pat Sears, 2020

1917

1950

1 DOWNTOWN
2 GARFIELD
3 DOUGLASS
4 CENTRAL
5 COLLEGE HIGH
6 JANE PHILLIPS
7 BOYS CLUB
8 SOONER HIGH
9 MADISON JR. HIGH

A FRANK PHILLIPS BLVD.
B VIRGINIA AVENUE
C 14TH STREET
D CHEROKEE AVENUE
E CANEY RIVER

1965

CHAPTER 8

MOODY'S REFUGE

In the 1960s, the slogan for the Boys Club nationally was "a place to go and a way to grow." For Ernest Guery, that place was the gym at the nearby Bartlesville Boys Club. Folks who knew Ernest often referred to him as "Moody," a reference to his frequently sullen facial expression. And in fact, Ernest could look quite serious, but the same people who called him Moody would tell you his smile "could light up a room." He made friends easily, and with his humility and modesty, had a way of putting everyone around him at ease. In addition to his older brother Larry, from whom Moody acquired a lot of his basketball skills, Ernest had a twin sister, Irma Linda. Friends of the Guery family remember Irma Linda, who stood nearly six feet tall, as much more demonstrative than her stoic twin brother.

As a youngster in a poor neighborhood, Ernest stayed close to home. When he wasn't in the house helping his mom take care of other children, he was in class at Douglass School just a block away, running errands, or playing basketball at the Boys Club. The place Ernie Jackson called "the club" was a refuge for many of Bartlesville's youth, particularly the underprivileged.

Moody prospered in that environment. His workout regimen at the Boys Club was legendary. He was solidly built and well-coordinated, but hardly a leaper. That wasn't enough for the junior high team at Central, where he missed the cut as a seventh grader. He was a member of the team the two following years, but played mostly as a reserve through the ninth grade. As part of the state championship AAU team in his final year at Central, he was able to blend the skills acquired from the long hours at the Boys Club with those of Phillips and other kids. They were coached that season by Madison science teacher Gene Williams, who provided a platform for Moody to advance his hoops career. Moving on to College High in the fall, he made the "B" team, or junior varsity his sophomore year, and was a part-time starter.

Author's note: Unfortunately, Ernest (Moody) Guery passed away in 2004 after a battle with cancer. Thus, this chapter lacks what others possess, i.e., firsthand accounts of growing up in Bartlesville. Rather, it provides more background on the significant influences of the community on Moody's family and friends.

Throughout junior high school, Moody and his friend Mike Louis continued to practice relentlessly on the playground and the Boys Club court. There was seldom a day when both didn't practice for hours. "Louie" was taller than Moody, growing to 6'3" by his high school days, and while he was a good shooter and ball handler, he lacked Moody's quickness and dedication to fundamentals. He could have been described as the "Will Rogers of offense," in that "he never met a shot he didn't like." Still, the two worked out together, challenging each other with every conceivable feint and juke. Seven days a week, all year long they fought each other for shots, blocks, and rebounds. They were often joined by several other friends, but it didn't matter—they could make the most of a two-man game as well.

Jo Allyn Lowe was the driving force behind Oklahoma's first Boys Club. An area native, Lowe attended Oklahoma A & M College, where he played both varsity basketball and tennis. Following his graduation from college in 1937, he returned to Bartlesville and worked at the YMCA until World War II broke out. He enlisted in the Navy as a chief petty officer and soon received a commission as an Ensign. Before deploying to the European Theater, he was promoted to Lieutenant (Junior Grade). At the war's end, Lowe returned to Bartlesville, married Margaret Lewis, started a family, and resumed his career of service to the city's youth at the local YMCA. In 1954, supported by pipeline magnate H. C. Price and numerous other civic leaders, Oklahoma's first Boys Club was established on the west side, with Lowe as its executive director.

For the next twenty-one years, under Lowe's tireless leadership, the Bartlesville Boys Club flourished as a place where boys of all races could gather for "guidance and worthwhile activities." In the process of running "the club," Lowe became known as one of the community's most admired and respected citizens.

Prior to the Boys Club's establishment, Bartlesville was typical of communities throughout the country. Blacks made up about six percent of the population and, by today's standards, accepted their second-class perception surprisingly well. In the presence of the white majority, they nearly always appeared courteous, well behaved, and humble. Their neighborhood, although stricken with poverty, was quiet and orderly. The residents attended their own churches, shopped in their own stores, and seemingly paid little attention to the people across the tracks—except of course when they worked in their homes and yards.

Boys Club fishermen

"The club offered a wide variety of sports, crafts, and other year-round recreational and social activities: basketball, pool (billiards), table tennis, archery, and much more. Significantly, it had a jobs program for youth, including cutting grass and other landscaping chores that allowed us to earn money. In general, it was a place where we could keep busy through engagement in interesting and productive activities and build on sense of self-worth and self-respect."

Ernie Jackson, 2020

To white residents at the time, and to those who recall it now, racial discrimination wasn't much of an issue. Due in large part to the oil boom and growing postwar prosperity, the citizens viewed themselves and their town as progressive. Still, there were visible signs of discrimination if one were to look. The short-lived local bus line featured signs that read "colored take seats at the rear." Only a few doctors saw Black patients, and then only after regular hours and through the back doors. The schools were the most obvious examples of segregation, and their situation was taken for granted by most of the city.

Racial inequity was a quiet subject, seldom discussed publicly, but revealed in detail in a book by Louise S. Robbins, *The Dismissal of Miss Ruth Brown*. In her carefully researched book, published in 2000, Ms. Robbins describes the firing of the town's longtime librarian, Ruth Brown, for actions found objectionable to many in the community. The cause for her dismissal, residents were told through newspapers and other accounts, was for her role in the circulation of subversive material. In 1950, that was a convenient cover story. It was the beginning of the "McCarthy era," when anti-communism raged at a fever pitch. Senator Joseph McCarthy, along with the U.S. House Un-American Activities Committee, provided a platform to speak out against suspected disloyal and subversive individuals and activities. Fueled by Bartlesville's American Legion Post and other civic organizations, a campaign was waged against Ms. Brown on a premise of disloyalty, while masking other reasons. In fact, what led to her firing was her affiliation with the Congress on Racial Equality, and some of her outward expressions in favor of integration. Specifically, she had invited two young African-American girls to the library's reading session, and taken two Black women with her to Hull's Drug store, where they sat together seeking food service. Both of these actions were considered unthinkable by a large portion of the populace, yet were masked by the public explanations for her dismissal. After evaluating accusations of "communist sympathizing" against Ms. Brown, one of Bartlesville's most respected attorneys,

Richard Kane, commented, "That was a coverup...because people were unwilling to express the real reason."

Phillips Petroleum Company and Cities Service were similar in many ways to companies found all over America. Their workforces were educated and mostly male, with clerical positions largely reserved for women. The men who worked in the many city office buildings wore suits and ties—and frequently hats—to work. Many lived within walking distance of the business district while others drove or carpooled. For a short time in the late '40s and early '50s a bus line provided limited service. The largely white-collar workforce could have easily been mistaken for IBM's, or any other prominent corporation.

Phillips wasn't exactly silent on the issue of race in Bartlesville. The company's workforce, which was entirely white, had employees and their spouses who took an active role in the case involving Ruth Brown. Following the retirement of Frank Phillips in 1949, Kenneth S. (Boots) Adams became the most influential person in town. Not only was he the company president, Adams was also a member of the American Legion Post, and served as president of the Chamber of Commerce. Through those organizations, it could easily be determined what the preferred, i.e. "Phillips," side of an issue was. The company had at its disposal a couple of "field activities" that became destinations for employees who crossed an imaginary line. One was a nuclear facility in Idaho Falls, Idaho, and the other a refinery in Borger, Texas, which Ms. Robbins described as the Phillips version of Siberia. More than a few of Ms. Brown's supporters faced the choices of remaining silent, being transferred, or resigning.

The full story of Miss Ruth Brown wasn't reported at the time, and even today isn't widely known by Bartians. Instead, life continued as usual in Bartlesville. Following the *Brown v. Board of Education* Supreme Court decision in 1954, the town moved to desegregate its school systems, although many schools remained segregated by neighborhood. The Caney River, running through the town, replaced the railroad tracks as an informal dividing line between white and Black schools. The community remained peaceful and generally affluent. At one point in the fifties, it boasted the highest percentage of college graduates per capita of any place in the world. On the downside, with desegregation bringing an end to Douglass School, the small nucleus of educated, middle-class Black adults began to dwindle.

CHAPTER 9

JUST PLAIN SID

Born and raised in Bartlesville, Sid Burton exemplified his hometown's work ethic. His father, Armand, named his only child Armand Sidney Burton, Jr., but called him Sid from birth. That year was 1933, and the Great Depression was winding down. While Sid's mother stayed home to take care of him, his father worked around town as a soda jerk, minding the counters at various shops and stores. Earning enough to live on was serious enough that Armand, at one point, packed the family car and headed for Texas. The stay was short-lived, though, as President Franklin D. Roosevelt's Works Progress Administration established a program five miles north of Bartlesville to create the new Bar-Dew Lake. Armand happily returned to his home town for promising employment. The family's life in Bartlesville was interrupted again in the early forties by World War II, when Armand was summoned to military duty—first in Fort Lauderdale, Florida, and then in San Francisco.

Virtually all of Bartlesville's families were disrupted in some way by the war, but the oil companies in general provided more stability in home lives. No one could boast harder working, more loving parents than Sid, and his father in particular went to great lengths to provide for his family. Eventually, long after Sid left town, Armand landed another job with the federal government, this time working as a mail handler at the local post office.

When not moving around, young Sid was an elementary school student at Garfield, and later attended Central Junior High School. Both of Sid's parents stressed the importance of school work, and Sid easily navigated his way through an exceptional school system. He was a scrappy kid, known for his competitive nature. At Garfield, Sid recalls being named the school's most outstanding athlete, by a narrow vote of four to two. He enjoyed sports year-round, immersing himself in football, basketball, baseball, and tennis. By the time he reached College High School, he located two enduring mentors—basketball coach Bailey Ricketts and baseball coach Burl Stidham.

Sid's senior year, 1948-49, was Stidham's first year in Bartlesville, and he was immediately impressed with the young Burton's "know-how." He never approached a job halfway, whether in the classroom or on an athletic field. Upon graduation from College High School in 1949, Sid left for Phillips University, a church-affiliated college in Enid, Oklahoma. At Phillips, he continuously carried a full course load, but also found time to excel as a three-sport athlete—a starter on the school's football, basketball, and baseball teams. It was also at Phillips, appropriately on the gymnasium steps, where he met his future bride, Jan. Together, they graduated in 1953 and Sid enlisted in the Army where he soon came to enjoy the service's sports programs.

"The most fun I had in the Army was getting out."
Sid Burton, March 2020

Sid and his young bride returned to Enid after three years, and there he launched his high school coaching career while earning a master's degree from Phillips. Armed with a second degree and two years of coaching experience, Sid received an offer from his high school alma mater, and returned to Bartlesville in 1958. He was immediately reunited with his former coach and mentor, Burl Stidham, who was in his tenth year of coaching College High School football. Sid was assigned classroom duties as a history teacher, and athletic responsibilities in football, basketball, and baseball, and was as happy as he was the day he got out of the Army!

Not only was Sid happy, but he immediately developed a legion of loyal, inspired followers in the classroom and locker rooms. Marty Lowe, one of four sons of Jo Allyn and Margaret, knew Sid as both a teacher and coach, and took time to recall in an essay what Sid meant to him:

"He was our teacher, our coach, our mentor, our confidant, our friend. Some of the guys referred to him as 'The Great Mentor.' I think some may have called him 'El Sid' as a play on the popular movie *El Cid* that starred Charlton Heston. Sid signed his Christmas cards to his players as 'Coach Sid Whistle Drills' and 'Jingle Bells Burton.' But to most of us he was, is, and will always be just Sid. Not Mr. Burton, not Coach Burton, but—Sid.

"I think he wanted us to call him that. It was not a case where 'he gave permission' or 'allowed' us students and players to call him by his first name. It was certainly not a case where we presumed ourselves to be equals and as such were 'entitled' to call him by his first name. It was just who he was—to himself and to us.

"Make no mistake that Sid was in charge and he made sure that was understood up front whether it was in the classroom, on the football or baseball field, or on the basketball court. All the activities were known for their decorum and order. He was there to teach and coach, and we were there to learn and execute from his instruction. BUT (and this is a rather large 'but'), we students and players were all people first in his eyes and he treated everyone with dignity and respect. As a result, we responded in kind towards him. Sid would never show you up in class if you didn't know an answer or performed poorly on a quiz. Likewise, he might call you out in a practice for general correction, but serious discussions were in private. Contrast that with some coaches who become irate at a player who makes a mistake, then get in their face and yell at them in front of the bench and crowd in a heated fashion, making a big scene out of it. So many times those chastised players end up playing 'not to make a mistake' instead of just playing. That was not an issue with Sid. EVER. So, in a way when we called him Sid instead of Mr. Burton or Coach Burton it was out of respect for him. We respected who he was. We respected how he treated us. We respected Sid.

"Sid and his lovely wife Jan were 'cool'. What do I mean? Well, they kept up with current fads, music, styles, and things that high school kids liked. Example: Jan Burton had a poster of The Beatles on the inside of the door to the storage closet in her classroom. In 1964 at a football practice I made contact with a receiver before the ball got there. Sid admonished me—in his outside voice—that if I did that in a game, the referee would not let me off without a flag even if I sang the chorus of 'Dang me,' a popular Roger Miller song at that time. They got all the references to things like the 'new' Batman television series or young peoples' slang terms. And they didn't just reject things out of hand like many adults of the day did. They would let you know if you had gone too far, but mainly just let kids 'do their thing.'

"Sid was excellent as a teacher. In the 1960s College High School had some of the most outstanding educators that one could imagine. More than one student made a 'perfect' score of 36 on the ACT (especially in math) standardized test. Our senior class of 1967 had over a dozen Merit Scholars. While we had some exceptionally bright students, the instruction (and encouragement) they received from the teaching faculty contributed greatly to the academic achievements of the students. Sid could match his knowledge and teaching ability in history to any of the teachers in English, math, foreign languages, art or any subject.

"Sid loved history and had the gift to convey that love to his students, and in some cases even transfuse that love to a student. He is a naturally vibrant fellow. No, Sid is an ebullient fellow! Ask anyone who ever knew Sid and they will tell you to a person that he is indeed 'bubbling over with enthusiasm.' Imagine a character with that type of energy, a booming voice, and a veritable boundless knowledge of history standing before you intent on imparting as much of that knowledge to you as he can. That was Sid in his classroom. I always liked history, but most of the kids could take it or leave it. Sid pretty much got everybody in his class to take it—and to really like it.

"Here is an example of American History learned from being in Sid's class. Have you ever heard of a frontier renegade by the name of Simon Girty? He led raids on frontier settlements in the late eighteenth and early nineteenth century. Sid told us about him and said a common 'threat' parents used back then to get kids to mind was to follow it by saying 'Simon Girty will get you!' 'If you don't get all those chores done before dinner, Simon Girty will get you!' 'If you don't stop talking right now and go to sleep, Simon Girty will get you!' That usually got a chuckle from the class. Then Sid in his brilliance would periodically throw it in during the year with statements like 'If you don't study for this next test, Simon Girty will get you!' or 'If you don't turn in your homework assignment on time, Simon Girty will get you!' I took American History under Sid in the 1965-66 school year. That was fifty-four years ago as I am writing this and I still remember Simon Girty (and that he will 'get me' if I don't do right!).

"You could talk to Sid (or Jan) about life or problems or just about anything. Sid would listen to you and hear what you were saying. Many adults wouldn't listen and some that listened to you did it in a patronizing way and really didn't want to hear what you said. Sid was different. Sid heard you—he really did! Sid was friendly toward you when he was your teacher or coach. Outside the class or off the field/court, he was your friend.

"Sid Burton was a teacher, a coach, a mentor, a confidant, a friend. He was one of a kind. Not Mr. Burton or Coach Burton, but just Sid. He was, is, and will always be—Sid."

The accolades for Sid don't end with Marty Lowe's. Jim Hess graduated from College High in 1961, and has lived in Bartlesville for a vast majority of the time since then. He owns a liquor store, "5th and Shawnee Discount Liquor," appropriately located at the corner of 5th and Shawnee, just a few blocks from the heart of downtown Bartlesville. From his modest store, Hess has long monitored the pulse of Bartlesville, and is regarded as somewhat of a local historian. He is well known and highly respected for his role in the College High School Alumni Association, having served as its chairman and the founder of the alumni scholarship program. Jim is an unabashed admirer of Sid Burton, and attributes his own lifelong love of history to the days spent in Sid's classroom. He recalls Sid pointing to Vietnam on a world map and telling the students to take note—that some of them would one day find themselves in that distant part of the world. Those words echo in Jim's mind to this day.

Don Wilber was another student of Sid's. Now retired from a successful career as an Oklahoma City area pediatrician, Dr. Wilber still remembers a long list of Civil War generals, taught to him and emphasized by Sid. Don knew Sid well, having grown up in the same church with the Burtons and serving as the student manager on the 1966-67 Wildcat basketball team. He went on to play for the varsity team the following year as a senior.

Likewise, Sue Reynolds has fond remembrances of Sid's classroom. Now a retired Bartlesville teacher, she counts herself as one of many students who was motivated by her American History teacher. She enjoyed a long and rewarding career in the Bartlesville school system, and made her mark on at least one future basketball star. Former University of Connecticut and NBA standout Emeka Okafor moved to Bartlesville as a youngster when his father was transferred there by Phillips Petroleum Company. Years later, recalling his time in

Bartlesville, he cited Mrs. Reynolds, his second grade teacher, as one of his all-time favorites.

Sid is remembered for far more than the classroom and the basketball court. He served several years as an assistant varsity football coach, and as head coach of the "B Team," or junior varsity. Additionally, he was the head varsity baseball coach throughout his time at College High School. Regardless of the sport, members of Sid's teams recall his commitment to conditioning. Indoors or out, Sid had no tolerance for carelessness or lack of hustle. Either would likely result in laps, wind sprints, or stair climbing, although they were sometimes amplified by heart-to-heart talks. He didn't curse or lose his cool, but he relied heavily on his whistle, resulting in being nicknamed "Whistle Drills" Burton by his basketball players. He happily acknowledged that moniker by having his Christmas cards engraved with that term of endearment.

Dave Selim, Class of '62, was best known as a local swimming stand-out. He recalls watching baseball practice and seeing Sid hit "unbelievable popups. He could hit them straight up to incredible heights." Brothers Stu and Bruce Bennett played baseball for Sid several years apart, and both recall the running he demanded at baseball practice.

Joe Troxell, who graduated in 1963, wrote, "He was a great role model. I don't remember him ever belittling anyone over anything. Sid could correct us in his calm way of communication. He made us a team." Troxell added that "Sid" is what they called him "and with great respect for he was greater than Mister." Troxell's classmate on that baseball team, Joe Dillsaver, remembers Sid as "one of the great influences" of his life.

Bill Turner and Vicki Ferraro graduated from College High in 1961 and attended the University of Oklahoma together. They wed in March 1964, and enjoy sharing their remembrances of Sid. Bill, who became a physician, played both football and baseball for Sid until he was urged to give up football. His coach wanted to protect him from injuries, calling Bill his "best left-handed pitcher ever." Bill has modestly suggested that he might have been Sid's only lefty. Vicki, like many of Sid's history students, became a teacher, and recalls the wonderful influence he had on all of his students.

It is clear that Sid was loved and respected by all who knew him, and being called "Sid" placed him on a higher level than anyone around him.

CHAPTER 10

BIG BROTHER IS WATCHING

College High School was built to accommodate both high school and junior college students in 1939. Its "streamline moderne" design, with striking white paint, created a picturesque setting on the twenty-acre site on South Hillcrest Drive. From its opening until the mid-fifties, the school consisted of two primary buildings—one with most of the classrooms, the other the field house, with a gymnasium and spaces for band, orchestra, and industrial arts classes. Then, as Bartlesville grew and integrated schools led to expanded enrollment, College High School added a third major building, Custer Stadium. It was more than a stadium, though, as underneath the seats were classrooms, teachers' offices, and locker rooms.

The field house was constructed with funds from the Frank Phillips Foundation, an appropriate gesture given that its gym became home to the Phillips 66ers basketball team, as well as the high school's Wildcats. There were backboards at the east and west ends of the court, and wooden bench seating rose upward from the court on both the north and south sides, seating about 1,100 spectators. There were doors near the corners along an otherwise solid wall at the west end, and a broad, elevated stage stood behind the east end backboard. It was a cozy but

Bartlesville College High School

Field House

comfortable setting for AAU and high school basketball—at least until the crowd warmed up.

There was no crowd when the Wildcats took the court for pre-season practice in November 1966. Temperatures had begun to drop outside as late autumn draped over northeast Oklahoma. There were very few leaves left on the trees around College High, and the north wind brought ominous signs of the coming winter. The seventy-five feet between the main building and field house created a slight wind tunnel, where anyone walking between them was sure to feel an occasional extra gust.

But that was outside. Inside the field house, the squeaking of sneakers, the pounding of balls, the beads of sweat, and the shrill blasts from Sid Burton's whistle created a virtual inferno. Fifteen superbly conditioned athletes competed for a coveted spot on the Wildcats' basketball team. Most knew from the start of practice that four starting positions were taken. Eagle, Sport, Moody, and Boody were returning starters from last season. Martindale was hurt, leaving an open competition for the fifth starting slot—and Sid would need at least seven reserves. Mike Louis, David Peterson, Steve Hale, and Bob Larson were all legitimate contenders, but there were no concessions from Jack Brown, Larry Houchin, Jim Bailey, and Mike Dershem. They were all juniors or seniors; they had been around for a while and knew Sid would give everyone a chance.

When the first players arrived on the court, there were a couple of bystanders on the stage overlooking the court. In the hall outside, beneath the north side's seats, another group of students visited quietly, oblivious to the players leaving the locker room for the court. Among the players were some sophomores—younger players who knew making the varsity team was a longshot, but who knew Coach Don Calvert's "B Team" would also play a full schedule of games.

Together, the twenty players ran up and down the court, and occasionally up and down the bleacher steps to the tune of Sid's commanding whistle. Twenty minutes into practice they were given a break. Their shirttails and tongues hanging out, they huddled around their coaches and managers for towels, water, and further instruction. Not fully rested, but responding to another of Sid's whistles, the players hustled back onto the court to resume their drills. Then, in a moment that neither will ever forget, Boody Sears and Moose Larson noticed a visitor near the doorway from the hall. He was someone they recognized immediately—not another student, not a teacher, and not a parent—it was a recent AAU All-American Phillips 66er, Denny Price. Boody and Moose didn't know what Price was doing in the College High School gym, but they knew at once that they didn't like it.

CHAPTER 11

THE PRICE FAMILY

If a title like "First Family of Oklahoma Basketball" could be bestowed on anyone, it might well be the family of William Dennis "Denny" Price and his wife, the former Ann Dunn. The family patriarch, Denny, achieved legendary status as a high school hoopster in Norman where, as a junior, he led his team to its first "big school" state championship by scoring a tournament record forty-two points on fifteen for eighteen shooting. That win, 60-59 over Bartlesville in 1955, would be remembered for a decade as one of the most thrilling tournament games ever played in Oklahoma. Price's scoring record held up until 1982, when his oldest son Mark matched it while playing for Enid.

Following the next season, in which he was named Oklahoma Player of the Year, Denny accepted a basketball-baseball scholarship to play at the nearby University of Oklahoma. He enjoyed a superb career at OU, earning all-Big Eight honors, graduating in 1960, and accepted an offer to play for the Phillips 66ers. In 1964, Ann gave birth to the first of their three sons, Mark, who would become a star at both the college and professional levels. Two more sons, Matt and Brent, followed, with Brent attaining college and NBA success. Mark would play for Enid High School, Georgia Tech, and primarily the

Cleveland Cavaliers, where he was a four-time all-star. Brent played two seasons for the University of South Carolina before transferring to the University of Oklahoma for his final two seasons. He followed an all-Big Eight season in 1992 with eleven seasons in the NBA.

Not to be forgotten in the Price family, the middle son, Matt, would play basketball at Appalachian State, and later at Phillips University in Enid, Oklahoma, where his father was head coach. Unfortunately, Matt had his basketball career abbreviated by two back injuries.

> *The legendary University of North Carolina coach, Dean Smith, knew the Price family well. He scouted Mark in high school in 1982, but recruited another Oklahoma guard, Steve Hale of Jenks High School instead of Price. As luck would have it, the day after Hale agreed to attend UNC, Jenks faced Enid in the state playoffs. Hale was regarded as one of the top defensive players in the country, a trait that clearly appealed to Dean Smith. With Smith in attendance, Price lit up the scoreboard with his record-tying 42 points, something Smith acknowledged years later by allegedly telling Mark Price, "I picked the wrong guy."*

Much of the Price family fame came later, but by 1966, Denny was well known both locally and nationally. He was known as a man of great faith and strong character, as well as a highly skilled athlete. Twice he was named an AAU All-American on a national championship team (1962 and 1963). Following his last season with the 66ers, he remained with the parent company, joining a stable of other former players who took their cues from the chairman, Boots Adams. Others in that group included Olympian Jerry Shipp, AAU All-American Charlie Bowerman, and former Texas Tech great Del Ray Mounts, each of whom had contributed in various ways to the basketball program at Central Junior High School. Nothing, however, in Price's experience had prepared the twenty-eight-year-old for the reception awaiting him at College High School, where Adams sent him in late 1966.

CHAPTER 12

THE TOWN'S OTHER TEAM

Robert Albert Kurland: A seven-footer. First two-time Olympic gold medal winner, the man whose shot-blocking resulted in a rule change, and the Phillips 66ers' most famous player.

As the College High School Wildcats prepared for their basketball season, Bartlesville's better known team, the 66ers, was launching what would be its penultimate season. Bob Kurland was long gone. In its first forty-five years, the team had won eleven national championships, produced thirty-nine All-Americans, twelve Olympians, and two Olympic head coaches. No team in the world could match those accomplishments. However, the makeup of the nation's amateur basketball programs had gradually changed over the past ten years, due in large part to competition from professional basketball. In the early fifties, even after the establishment of the National Basketball Association, there were attractive reasons why the best college players chose AAU teams over the pros. Large companies like Phillips could offer the players jobs that paid salaries comparable to the NBA's, and Phillips in particular had a strong track record of success for its former players. Many went on to executive positions, and young recruits were pointed toward the millionaire status that several ex-players had achieved. In the fifties and early sixties, that was viewed as "real money."

Notable Phillips 66ers:

Bob Kurland—Helms Foundation National Player of the Year (1946), two national championships at Oklahoma A&M (1945 and 1946), six-time AAU All-American

Bud Browning—USA Olympic basketball coach (Gold Medal, 1948), seven-time AAU national champion coach

Gerald Tucker—Helms Foundation National Player of the Year (1947), USA Olympic basketball coach (Gold Medal, 1956)

Even following superstar Bob Kurland's playing career, recruiting exceptional college players continued. Some were nationally known without the aid of television. For example, Kurland's final season, 1951-52, coincided with the first of Clyde Lovellette's two seasons. Lovellette had a remarkable pedigree, having attended high school in the basketball hotbed state of Indiana, followed by a college career under legendary coach Phog Allen at Kansas. As a Jayhawk, he was a teammate of future coaching legend Dean Smith, and was named national college player of the year in 1952. As perhaps a sign of things to come, the six-foot nine-inch star left Phillips after two seasons to join the Minneapolis Lakers of the NBA. Over the next eleven seasons, Clyde was named as an all-star three times, and contributed to three championships—one with the Lakers and two with the Celtics.

Lovellette might have been the most famous Indiana high school player on a Phillips roster, but the state produced another hoop hero in Bobby Plump. A native of tiny Milan, Indiana, Plump came to Bartlesville via Butler University in 1958. Four years earlier he led his underdog high school team to the state championship in the game remembered by many as Indiana's greatest sports moment, and one that inspired the 1986 sports movie, *Hoosiers*. Based loosely on Milan's season, the film features a game-winning shot by the fictional Jimmy Chitwood, who in real life was Bobby Plump.

Plump, who stood only 5'11", was joined on that 1958 Phillips team by another small town product, 6'5" forward Jerry Shipp, who was raised in Blue, Oklahoma. Shipp wasn't well known coming out of Southeast Oklahoma State, but earned enough national attention in five years as a 66er to be named to the 1964 U. S. Olympic team. There, under coaching legend Henry Iba, Shipp was not only the team's captain, but the leading scorer as the U.S. won the gold medal. That team featured such future NBA all-stars as Bill Bradley, Walt Hazzard, and Jim Caldwell.

Those Phillips teams of the late fifties and early sixties wouldn't have been complete, or nearly as successful, without a final player from a really small town. Like Milan and Blue, Roland, Iowa, was barely a spot on the map. But also like the other towns, Roland produced a basketball legend. Known as the "Roland Rocket," the 5'10" kid with a crew cut attended Iowa State University. It was there that Gary Thompson would become an All-American in both basketball and baseball, and be chosen Big Seven Player of the Year over Kansas great Wilt Chamberlain. After a sterling college career, and being drafted by the Minneapolis Lakers in 1957, Thompson opted for the AAU's Phillips team.

Phillips 66ers championships:

National AAU (eleven) 1940, 1943-48, 1950, 1955, 1962-63

National Industrial Basketball League (eleven) 1949-58, 1960

The next eleven years brought a wide range of emotions to Thompson. The 66ers continued to enjoy great success and Thompson experienced the fame that accompanied it. Within a year he was playing on Team USA with fellow backcourt legends Jerry West and Oscar Robertson. He became the 66ers' captain and led them to national AAU championships in 1962 and '63. In 1962 he was named the tournament's most valuable player. Two years after those championship seasons, Gary was named the 66ers' head coach, replacing the legendary Bud Browning. Unfortunately for Thompson and the team, the NBA had gained in visibility and prominence, and also in the amount of money teams could offer their recruits. It wasn't always about the money either. Thompson talked about trying to bring a nationally known player, Larry Brown, to Bartlesville. Brown had played for coaching legends Frank McGuire and Dean Smith at North Carolina, and while small at 5'9", had played well enough to make the 1964 gold medal-winning Olympic team. At the same time, Brown was also playing for the AAU's Akron Goodyear Wingfoots, leading them to the 1964 national championship. It was during his Akron stint that Thompson learned of Brown's interest in "the oil business," which meant playing for Phillips. After some brief conversations, Brown decided against going to Bartlesville, saying he wasn't sure the place was ready for a Jewish ballplayer.

Whether Brown's Jewish heritage was a problem or not, it was a surprise to Thompson. The question of a player's religion had never arisen in his time with Phillips, but the company did have rigorous standards for employment. Engineers were hired from the top ten percent of their college classes and all employees were held to high standards of conduct and appearance. Ballplayers were no different— they had real "day jobs" in addition to their practices and games schedules. It was believed that during his tenure, Clyde Lovellette failed to take the day job as seriously as he did the basketball, accounting in part for his brief time with the team.

Throughout the existence of its basketball team, both the company and team projected an all-white image. UCLA great Walt Hazzard was rumored to be a Phillips candidate about the same time as Larry Brown, but the results indicate that the company wasn't ready, for whatever reason, to change its team's racial makeup. Thompson continued to seek top-level college talent, trying a year later to recruit Rick Barry, Gail Goodrich, twins Dick and Tom Van Arsdale, Billy Cunningham, and Fred Hetzel, hoping he could get one of them. By then, sadly for Phillips and amateur basketball everywhere, the pull of the NBA had become too strong. All of those Phillips targets became successful professional players and the end for Phillips basketball was looming.

The team's presence in the community wasn't limited to company time. There were clear signs of Phillips' involvement throughout the community. In addition to providing monetary support to the school system, YMCA and YWCA, and the Boys Club, the company encouraged all of its employees to volunteer in local activities. Basketball players were particularly visible in youth sports leagues. Joe Dean, a 66er in the mid-fifties, served as an assistant coach for a Little League team sponsored by the Lions Club. Dean left Phillips for a lucrative job with Converse, and many years later was named athletic director at Louisiana State University.

Gary Thompson called on his college baseball experience to assist with a Pony League team whose sponsor was the Frank Phillips Men's Club. At least two other 66ers, Charlie Bowerman and Denny Price, coached Phillips dependents in a youth basketball program. They and others were sometimes seen at local schools, either as observers or volunteer coaches. What their responsibilities were and who sent them weren't always clear, although Bowerman recalls being sent to Central Junior High School by Phillips Chairman Boots Adams to see if he could "help out the coaches." There were frequent discussions around town about how much of that "help" was actually welcome.

Such was the local landscape in late 1966 when the 66ers and Wildcats prepared to open their seasons.

1963-64 Phillips 66ers
Back: Mgr Don Watkins, Jerry Shipp, Ken Charlton, Jim Hagan,
Mike Moran, Tony Cerkvenik, Coach Bud Browning
Front: Ken Saylors, Del Ray Mounts, Denny Price, Larry ·
Pursiful, Charlie Bowerman, Bob Turner

Phillips Petroleum Company
Chronology of Leadership

Frank Phillips: President from incorporation in 1917 until 1938 (Age 65); Chairman of the Board until 1949

Kenneth S. (Boots) Adams: Named President in 1938; remained as Chief Executive Officer until 1964 (Age 65); Chairman of the Board until 1968; remained as board member until 1970

Paul Endacott: Elected President in 1951; Vice-Chairman of the Board 1962-1967 (Age 65)

Stanley Learned: Elected President in 1962, replacing Endacott; became CEO in 1964, replacing Adams; retired in 1967 (Age 65)

John Houchin: President in 1968, Chairman of the Board 1968-1974 (Age 65)

William Keeler: Chief Executive Officer, 1968-1973 (Age 65)

William F. (Bill) Martin: Senior Vice-President of Executive Committee 1965, Executive Vice-President in 1968, President in 1971, Chairman and CEO 1974-1982 (Age 65)

J. (Pete) Silas: Senior Vice-President in 1978; Executive Vice-President in 1980; President in 1982

Titles such as President, CEO, and Chairman may be ambiguous to readers today, but they were clear to the officers who bore them. Key ones are highlighted as follows:

President: Frank Phillips 1917-1938, Boots Adams 1938-1951, Paul Endacott 1951-1962, Stanley Learned 1962-1968, John Houchin 1968-1971, Bill Martin 1972-1982, C. J. (Pete) Silas 1982 and beyond

Chairman of the Board: Frank Phillips until 1949; Boots Adams 1949-1968; John Houchin 1968-1974, Bill Martin 1974 until 1982

Names underscored are former Phillips 66ers basketball players.

Notes of interest:

William Keeler was also the last appointed and first elected Principal Chief of the Cherokee Nation.

Adams, Endacott, Learned, and Keeler were all University of Kansas alumni. Houchin and Martin graduated from the University of Oklahoma, Silas from Georgia Tech.

Martin and Houchin had sons (Scott and Larry) who were members of the 1966-67 Wildcat basketball team.

CHAPTER 13

AVERTING A CRISIS

Boody and Moose weren't the only Wildcats who saw Denny Price standing by the court that afternoon. One of their classmates, Monty Johnson, was in the gym and will never forget seeing Price and imagining what he was doing. All three concluded that the recent 66er star was there on a mission from headquarters.

Boots Adams retired as president of Phillips at the age of sixty-five in 1964, after leading the company for twenty-seven years. He remained with the company as its board chairman and a year later was feted to an extravagant celebration of his sixty-sixth birthday. Called "Celebration 66," the party featured a downtown parade with former President Dwight Eisenhower as the grand marshal, and a flyover by the U.S. Air Force "Thunderbirds." Their thunderous appearance under low overcast skies was completed just before a daylong downpour tried but failed to halt the festivities. Stanley Learned, another Kansas alumnus, had replaced Adams as president, but August 31, 1965, reminded everyone in Bartlesville that Adams was still the town's biggest name.

Boots Adams at his desk

Boots Adams' office was located in downtown Bartlesville, less than a mile and a half from the high school. It was a spacious office—welcoming and not ostentatious—with a view of downtown on two sides and a picture of Frank Phillips on the wall to the side of his desk. From there, Boots was known to dispatch "helpers" to the local schools, particularly Central Junior High and College High Schools. Everyone in town knew of Boots' interest in sports. From his days at Kansas to the creation of the Phillips 66ers, Adams established himself as a "sports guru." His son from his first marriage, Kenneth S. (Bud) Adams, Jr., was born and raised in Bartlesville, and by 1960 was the founder and owner of the Houston Oilers professional football team. Bud Adams, along with Lamar Hunt, is credited with leading the establishment of the American Football League in the sixties.

Boots had two daughters, Stephanie and Lisa, and three other sons by his second marriage. Steve, Ken, and Gary attended Central Junior High School and College High School in the sixties, and all were exceptional, well-rounded young men—solid students and good athletes. Boots, like most fathers, was keenly interested in his sons' development, but unlike most fathers, he had extraordinary means at his disposal to provide assistance—not necessarily to his sons, but to the teams at the schools they attended.

> *"In 1963-64, the coach that Bowerman along with Shipp and Mounts helped was Dorsey Gibson. Gibson was brought in by Phillips that year to coach football and basketball at Central. He did not teach anything at Central. The move by Phillips in the summer of 1963 led to the resignation of previous coach Charles Witty, who left town and moved to Bristow to become a teacher and coach there—without any corporate 'assistance.' Word has it he was 'mad as hell' about what Phillips was doing at that time."*
> Marty Lowe, 2020

In 1966, longtime College High football coach Bill Holbrook was quietly transferred to Sooner High School to make room for a Phillips favorite, Tom Turvey. Holbrook had been an assistant under Burl Stidham until he replaced him following the 1961 season. He was an exceedingly popular coach and teacher, and the move to replace him with Turvey was universally unpopular. It was also ineffective, as football/basketball players such as Ernie Jackson, Pat Sears, Scott Martin, and Bob Larson saw their football fortunes turn sour after a promising first month of the season. So what was the cause of their angst? It was twofold. First, there was a natural and understandable discomfort with a coach who had replaced a popular and respected leader. Some didn't like his style. Second, since coaches weren't involved in the hiring and shuffling process, there were at least latent hard feelings toward whomever called the shots. Teenage boys didn't concern themselves with the politics of such decisions. There was not alarm—just the eager anticipation of basketball season and the opportunity to play once again for Sid Burton.

> *Cecil Epperly, who coached Wildcat basketball in the late sixties, recalls being told, "Be careful who's watching practice. The Phillips Executive Committee could be holding a meeting in the bleachers." There was a time when at least three top executives had sons on his team.*

Then, the alarm went off. When a recent Phillips player showed up in the gym, practice couldn't end quickly enough for at least two of the players. Denny Price's appearance had been brief but consequential. There was a passing mention of it in the locker room following practice, with Boody holding back his thoughts, telling only Moose Larson that he was going to see Burl Stidham in the morning. To Boody, Burl stood above everyone he knew as a voice of reason. He had retired from active coaching five years earlier, and was named athletic director of Bartlesville City Schools. Even his time as athletic director was behind him—Burl was simply a teacher and friend, but also one who was familiar with Phillips' "shenanigans." He was short in stature, but long in experience and confidence, the qualities Boody was seeking when he knocked at Burl's door. At age fifty-six, the 5'8" history teacher and former coach provided a warm welcome to Boody when he stepped into his office. Burl was like a father figure to Boody, but maybe even easier to talk with. It didn't take Boody long to tell Burl why he was there—Phillips was making another run on the school system's coaches, and this one was hitting close to home. Burl's face revealed concern—Boody would learn many years later of Burl's history with Phillips—but his mentor chose his words carefully. Leaning back in his chair and gazing past Boody toward the hall outside, Burl slowly but firmly said, "Follow your heart." Burl seemed to know where Boody's heart would lead him, but offered no further advice, simply adding, "You'll know what is right."

CHAPTER 14

A CALL TO ACTION

"Help!" by The Beatles. The words to the Beatles' 1965 hit song were stuck in Boody's brain—an earworm of the highest order. Without hesitation, he and Moose reached out to their fathers.

Life had been good to Swede Larson and G.O. Sears. Both had stable families, comfortable homes, and good, secure jobs with Phillips Petroleum Company. Both had sons at College High School—popular students who were three-sport varsity athletes. Moose Larson and Boody Sears played football and basketball together, and were close friends away from sports. Sid Burton tended to think of them as his cutups—his challenges for keeping his basketball team serious and focused. Sometimes that wasn't easy. Both Moose and Boody liked to have fun—sometimes even at the coach's expense. That could lead to increased attention—probably what they were looking for—and sometimes Sid's famous "whistle drills" where they would run up and down the court or repeatedly up and down the rows of seats lining the sides of the gym.

Swede and G.O. were greeted by much more serious looks on their sons' faces when they got home from practice on Friday. Boody had visited Burl Stidham and was now following his advice—and his own heart. He and Moose had agreed to take action, and they needed to enlist their fathers' help. Each told their dad about the previous day's practice, about Boody's meeting with Burl, and their growing determination to nip the Phillips overreach in the bud. Sure, they admired and respected Denny Price, but they had insurmountable loyalty to Sid, and they had no stomach for outside interference.

The two fathers, hearing their sons' stories separately, were convinced that their help was critical. The boys were distressed and needed support, and they were wise enough to ask the right people. Seldom has adult supervision been more essential. G.O. and Swede spoke by phone and decided to involve another leader in the process, and quickly enlisted the aid of Swede's neighbor and friend, Jo Allyn Lowe. Long aware of similar tactics by Phillips, Lowe agreed to help, and accepted an invitation to meet at the Larsons' house on South Johnstone Avenue.

After dinner that night, G.O. and Boody Sears drove across town to meet Moose and his dad, along with Jo Allyn. The five of them walked downstairs to the Larsons' basement and discussed writing a letter to local school authorities. Paul Geymann, who had replaced Burl Stidham as the school system's athletic director the previous year, would be the target of their communications. Not that it really mattered to them, but they were reasonably certain that Phillips bypassed Geymann in their coaching endeavors. One of the adults suggested that copies be provided to school Principal John Haley, Coach Sid Burton, and football coach Tom Turvey.

Boody, with the other four looking over his shoulder, wrote the letter—first by hand and later typing it. The letter was direct but courteous—carefully omitting some of the heated rhetoric the boys espoused. "If we want this to be effective," Jo Allyn said, "we need to keep it rational. Don't give them a reason to throw it away." With everyone in agreement, the letter was finalized and quickly circulated to the rest of the team for signatures. Everyone on the team agreed without hesitation to sign the draft copy. When a smoother version was circulated, the letter failed to reach Scott Martin for his signature. While no one can explain the omission with certainty, Boody surmised that the team's seniors had concern for Scott's unique position as the son of a Phillips executive, i.e., a father more susceptible to negative fallout should the "powers that be" get rankled (or get their undershorts in a knot). It would be a lot longer fall for Bill Martin than for G.O. Sears or Swede Larson.

John Haley
Copies: Tom Turver
        Sid Barton

November 20, 1956

Mr. Paul Geymann
Director of Athletics
Bartlesville, Oklahoma

Dear Mr. Geymann:

It is the general opinion of the undersigned players that Sid Barton should be given the sole responsibility of coaching the varsity basketball team without the help of outside individuals.

We as players feel that this is not an unjust desire. We feel that the team spirit and morale is in a very depressed state when the presence of outside help is felt.

The undersigned players realize that the help is intended for our benefit, but we feel that it is doing more harm in the way of morale and spirit let down than the good that comes about from the learning of more technique.

We would sincerely appreciate your thoughtful consideration of this request.

Yours truly,

1. Jim Bailey
2. E.J. Barnes
3. Jack Brown
4. Mike Denham
5. Richard Edgar (mgr.)
6. Ernest Huery
7. Steve Hale
8. Larry Houchin
9. Esme Jackson
10. Bob Parson
11. Michael Louis
12. Pat McCullough
13.
14. Craig Mattindale
15. David Peterson
16. Jim Powell
17. Pat Sears

CHAPTER 15

TIMEOUT FOR A WORD
FROM THE AUTHOR

Paul Eugene Geymann was new to Bartlesville and its school system. A Kansas native, he had attended Oklahoma A&M where he was a pole vaulter and a member of Henry Iba's national championship basketball team in 1946—a teammate of future Phillips 66er and Olympian Bob Kurland. Following college, Paul coached high school basketball in Topeka, Kansas, and Enid, Oklahoma, and then served as an assistant coach at the University of Oklahoma and the University of Missouri. In 1965, he was named athletic director of the Bartlesville school system, replacing the popular Burl Stidham. While it wasn't clear at the time, Geymann's actions over time revealed both a clear Phillips connection and an agenda.

To understand the events of November 1966 requires knowing more about some complex relationships. In Paul Geymann's college years, Bob Kurland was a "big man on campus" in more than one way. Notably, he was a seven-footer, a student who stood out wherever he went. For his ability on the basketball court, he was known from Stillwater, Oklahoma, to Madison Square Garden in New York, and from Olympic sites in London to Helsinki. He carried the American flag at the opening ceremony in Helsinki in 1952, and became the first athlete to win gold medals in successive Olympics. Twice he was named the Most Outstanding Player of the NCAA's Final Four.

Kurland, who was regarded as the consummate "gentle giant," was as humble and soft-spoken on the campus as he was dominant on the court. In both 1945 and 1946, he was elected president of A&M's student council. Phillips sent him to graduate school at Stanford, and he rose through the company's ranks as a highly effective marketing representative. In later years, long after his playing days, Bob would become Bartlesville's vice-mayor and a member of the city commission. For everything he brought to Phillips, he was clearly a favorite of Boots Adams—and one of the few people Geymann knew when he arrived in Bartlesville. While it's clear that Geymann and Kurland were college teammates, there is no indication of any connection between them later. Kurland steered clear of Bartlesville school affairs.

Geymann's predecessor as athletic director of the school system was Burl Stidham. Sid Burton and Burl were close friends who had a lot in common. Burl arrived in Bartlesville and became College High's football and baseball coach in 1948, Sid's senior year. Burl soon became an Oklahoma coaching legend, spending the next fourteen years as a winning coach, compiling a record of 180 wins, sixty-three losses and eleven ties in twenty-one years in Poteau, Panama, and Bartlesville. He retired from coaching after the 1961 season, but remained employed as a teacher and athletic director. He was succeeded as head football coach by Bill Holbrook.

Both Holbrook and Burton had been assistants under Burl, and a great sense of loyalty and friendship existed among the three of them. Burton's association with Burl went beyond their football ties, though, as both were American History teachers, were married to teachers, and belonged to the same church. Both were respected and admired throughout the school and the community, and it was difficult to know one without thinking of the other. Their loyalty could not be overstated, but it was eventually put to the test.

Bill Holbrook, Sid Burton, and Burl Stidham

When Geymann replaced Stidham in 1965, little was known about the circumstances surrounding the change. Even less was said at the time, but there was plenty of speculation. The fifty-five years since then haven't added clarity, but recently disclosed details have provided reasonable room for conjecture. It appears, from Geymann's earliest actions, that his marching orders were to "clean up after Burl." At the top of that list was "start with the coaches."

Note: *To be clear, the preceding paragraph is conjecture; the following one is not.*

One of Geymann's early moves was to hire a new football coach to replace Bill Holbrook, who was somewhat abruptly reassigned to a new school in the same district. The replacement, Tom Turvey, came from Oklahoma State University, and was reported to be a favorite of "Phillips brass." That move wasn't lost on Sid Burton, although he remained tight-lipped about the details for over fifty years, finally disclosing them while being interviewed for this book. On March 10, 2020, Sid, in a meeting with former players Pat Sears and David Peterson, along with their classmate Marty Lowe and the author, revealed a short but monumental history between Geymann and himself. As Sid recalled it, he met with Geymann in 1965, and among other things, expressed his dissatisfaction with the way his friend and former boss, Burl Stidham, had been treated. According to a conversation between Stidham and Burton, Stidham had received a call from a high-placed Phillips source, an emissary for company chairman Boots Adams. The essence of the call was to express displeasure that a Black football player was running back all the kicks and that Stidham should "tell Holbrook to get a white player in there." In all of Stidham's fifty-five years, nothing had prepared him for a moment like that. Local schools had been integrated for over ten years, and he had coached numerous Black athletes. The last thing he expected when he answered the phone that afternoon was to hear an order of a racial nature from the city's best known and strongest voice. Burl's reported reply was "maybe you should tell him that yourself." Stidham was soon relieved of his duties and eventually replaced by a new hire—Paul Eugene Geymann. Adams' messenger—known to Stidham and suspected by Burton—remains unnamed.

These events were understandably hard on Sid. At age thirty-five—just two years into a long-awaited head coaching job— he saw his mentor, Burl Stidham, fired, and his close friend, Bill Holbrook, reassigned.

The following summer, well after the 1965-66 basketball season, Geymann and Burton had another memorable conversation. Geymann indicated that it was his responsibility to review Sid's contract for the coming year, and at one point asked, "You do know who brought me here, don't you?" Burton replied that he assumed it was the local school board, to which Geymann said, "No, it was Phillips, the same people that dealt with Burl." Whether or not that was intended as a threat, a signal of "one-upmanship," or just a casual comment, it didn't sit well with Burton. His immediate reaction, which he shared only with his wife Jan, was "there's no need to review my contract. I'm not staying here." His gut feeling was that "if they got rid of Burl, they can certainly do the same thing to me. They're probably already thinking about a new starting lineup." However, he had another year before his GI loan eligibility expired, and he had a great group of basketball players anticipating the next season. After an intense struggle within himself, loyalty to his team prevailed, and Sid chose to remain their coach unless he was forced out. It's important to note that Sid didn't mention any of this to his players, but they would later develop their own reasons for concern about their mentor. Sid was left to ponder his future, and, at age 35, what would almost certainly be his final year at College High School.

Contrary to long-held opinions about Sid's situation, he was completely unaware of Denny Price's visit. The two didn't meet or talk to each other. To this day it isn't clear whether there was a connection between Price and Geymann. The players, unaware of Burton-Geymann discussions, knew simply that Paul Geymann was the one who could—and should—blow the whistle on Phillips' interference.

Personal note: Burl Stidham was more to me than a coach and teacher. He was my neighbor from the time I was two until I reached fourteen. Burl and his wife Lillian lived on the same block—several doors down and across the street— and we attended the same church. They were a couple you couldn't help but notice. Burl stood about 5'8"; Lillian appeared to be around 5'11". They were respected as great teachers and admired for being wonderful people.

When Sid Burton told four of us the story of Burl's dismissal, I admit to being brought to tears. I held them until the flight home, when thinking of the incident overwhelmed me. When he was told that a football player shouldn't play a prominent role on the team, simply because of the color of his skin, it was tough to swallow. Not unbelievable, not incomprehensible—just something I had never imagined. My heart went out to one of the finest men I had ever known. Burl was only fifty-five when that happened, and would live another thirty-six years bearing the weight of that experience.

Soon, as I began retelling the story, I heard comments like "that's not surprising; we came to expect things like that from Phillips." Or "everyone knew 'so-and-so' was a racist." In researching this book that was the "wow moment" for me—one that continues to haunt me today.

CHAPTER 16

ALL HANDS ON DECK

Moose Larson and Boody Sears delivered the letter to Geymann's office before morning classes began on Monday. They also hand-carried the copies to the school office and put them in the mail slots of Principal John Haley and coaches Sid Burton and Tom Turvey. It was still before lunchtime when Geymann read the letter and decided to act quickly. His plan included a visit with the team before their afternoon practice.

Despite his unpleasant encounters with Sid, Paul Geymann was widely regarded as a "nice guy"—fair, open-minded, and congenial—a guy who wanted the best for the young students in Bartlesville. He reread the letter from the team and needed immediate answers to what brought it on.

The afternoon couldn't pass quickly enough for Geymann. There was other work to do, but he couldn't focus on it. When he finally arrived at the College High School field house, it was 2:25 and a handful of players had begun making their way toward the court. Geymann was met by junior guard Larry Houchin, who asked how he could help. Letter in hand, Geymann showed it to Houchin, who had signed it a few days earlier. The youthful Houchin was like many of his teammates, blissfully unaware of any details behind the letter—just a guy who wanted his coach to be left alone. Within seconds, Moose Larson appeared from the locker room and Houchin introduced him to his new friend, Mr. Geymann. Moose assessed the situation immediately and led both of them, plus three other players near the scorer's table, to the stage overlooking the east end of the basketball court. Then, as two of them started pulling some gigantic sliding doors closed to give them privacy, Moose motioned for other players to join them on the stage. Boody Sears was one of the next players onto the court, and he helped by urging others to quickly follow him up the steps. Within minutes, all the players were there, although Sid remained in the locker room.

Moose and Boody, as drafters of the signed letter, were the first to speak. Geymann didn't have time to ask a question before Sears got straight to the point. "Mr. Geymann," he started, "if you and the school board want College High to have a basketball team this season, you need to let Sid Burton coach it."

"Yeah," added Larson. "And that means without any help—from anyone!"

There were head nods and murmurs of agreement from around the circle of players in their practice gear. No one else said anything. No one had to. Geymann seemed to understand as he acknowledged their comments. It's doubtful that he knew the extent to which Phillips was involved, but he was learning quickly. He needed to stop whatever the company was doing if College High were to have a basketball team. He left the gym quietly before Coach Burton arrived, and the players returned to their shoot-around.

Paul Geymann was inducted into the Bartlesville Sports Hall of Fame in 2015. He was recognized for his leadership in establishing girls' athletic teams in the schools before it was mandated by Title IX, and for many other achievements as the school system's director of athletics.

Intermission

In the Eye of the Storm

It's unquestionably overstating it to compare the conditions around the Wildcats to a hurricane, but the similarities are too real to ignore. Around the team, geographically and chronologically, significant events were brewing.

Predating the 1966-67 season the high school enjoyed a history of anticipating basketball prosperity. Perhaps fueled by the legendary Phillips 66ers—perhaps by the Wildcats' occasional but limited postseason success—students and players expected victories. In 1961, for example, the pep squad, cheerleaders, and student body bonded around the sing-song chant during timeouts at games: "Come along and bring your Wildcat cheer; we're going to go to 'State' this year." Occasionally they went to "State"—more often they didn't, but they *always* wanted to. It was that kind of town. As recently as 1962 and 1963, the 66ers were winning national AAU championships and making the town proud—at least most of the town.

Life was still quiet in Bartlesville's "colored town," as a number of the city's white people called it. Eagle, Moody, and Louie would frequently walk home together in the dark winter hours after practice. Occasionally they would get a ride, but only with friends. No strangers would pick them up and venture into their side of town. It wasn't because they viewed it as unsafe—it was just unfamiliar to them. The boys arrived at home to find happy and loving, but struggling families. Miss Mazie continued to spend long hours caring for neighborhood children while their parents worked in homes and yards across the tracks. Bettye Jackson found a second job—working the night shift at the nearby Reda Pump factory. Ernie, to whom she gave great strength and received steadfast love and admiration in return, was her protector. Ever mindful of his mother's safety, he would walk her to work on those cold, dark Oklahoma nights. Ernie's father, "Black Jack," had passed away three years earlier, leaving Ernie with greatly increased responsibility at home.

Yes, life was relatively tranquil inside the eye-wall. Outside, trouble was raging. During the junior year of Eagle, Louie, Moody, and others, Los Angeles fell victim to racial unrest with the infamous Watts riots. Before the team's junior class would graduate, Martin Luther King, Jr., would be assassinated, and that would be followed shortly by the shooting death of Robert Kennedy. That same year, 1968, would mark the Tet Offensive, a major escalation of a divisive war overseas.

But trouble like that hadn't reached Bartlesville in the fall of 1966—at least not on that scale. On their quiet walks home, the team's three Black players would sometimes muse about their experiences— pleasant and otherwise. Their conversations were like every other kid's—about school, girls, their teachers, what was going on at the club. But every now and then, the conversation drifted to race. Ernie provides a gripping account of some of those trying times:

"Yes, I was indeed called the n-word on several occasions during those years, but probably not as much as my peers. There are a couple of instances that stand out in my mind for very particular reasons. My elementary school days at St. John were generally free from the overt racism and discrimination experienced by the other Black kids who moved on from Douglass School to the surrounding all-white elementary schools. This, I believe, is likely because as a Catholic school, the priests, nuns, and lay teachers were some of the most racially progressive adults in the Bartlesville community and set the tone for a progressive school environment. So, I was never called the n-word at St. John—with one exception.

"When I was a third or fourth grader, a white male student a year behind me (I'll call him by his initials, PC) called me the n-word at least a couple of times on the playground and would take off running. I'd chase him but never caught him, and it's probably a good thing that I didn't because I can't say what I would have done to him although

I know it wouldn't have been good. Although the word stung, what bothered me most was that it had occurred at St. John, a place I felt was a haven and refuge from that sort of thing. It seemed to me that PC had violated the sanctity of the place as much as he had personally insulted me. He was by all measures a poor white kid—probably poorer than I was—who without doubt had his own economic, social, and cultural challenges. It was clear from his overall conduct and performance at school that he was enduring his own struggles, so in truth I really didn't hold him entirely responsible. I never saw him again after that year, and assumed that he and his family had moved on.

"Another incident that occurred my sophomore year is noteworthy because of its direct connection to my high school basketball career. During that year a few of us sophomores were called up to play with the varsity, and traveled with the team to play in a tournament in Sapulpa. Charlie Randle, a Black three-sport star at Col Hi who was a few years ahead of me and a good friend, had told me about his experiences with racism when playing in some of the smaller towns. The hometown fans in some of those places would sometimes call him things like the n-word, Snowflake, and so forth. So I was ready for just about anything alongside those lines.

"Since we had arrived at the Sapulpa gym in the early afternoon and didn't play until that evening, we watched the hometown team play its game. I noticed that Sapulpa had a few Black players so figured there'd be no problem with its fans. After that game a few of us, including me and Boody, decided to find some place nearby to eat. About four blocks from the gym we found a little establishment that appeared to be part restaurant and diner. It was filled with what appeared to be working class whites, but not a single Black person. A waitress took us to a larger back room where there was enough seating for us all. After a pleasant meal we went back to the front area to pay at the register and go back to the gym. When we got to the register I was the last in line behind Boody. As I looked around I saw two white guys probably in their early to mid-twenties in a booth near the register and the door.

The larger one looked at me, and in a voice loud enough for everyone to hear, said to the other: 'Ya know, I didn't know they start letting n——s eat in here!' There was dead silence. And by that time it was Boody's turn to pay, but he was so nervous he had problems getting his money out of his pocket. I quietly but firmly said, 'Pat, would you please hurry up and pay these people so we can get out of here?!'

"After paying we walked outside and crossed the street, intending to get back to the gym as soon as possible. Just then several men, including the two in the booth, appeared on the sidewalk in front of the restaurant. One of them yelled at us, 'Hey you boys! Come back here!' At that we took off running back to the gym as fast as our young legs could carry us. Later whenever I'd recount the incident, I'd often say jokingly in reference to my teammates that that was the first time I'd ever been outrun by white boys!

"But in all seriousness, I often thought about a likely connection between the elementary school incident with PC and the encounter at the Sapulpa restaurant. What would cause a child like PC to feel that he was entitled to demean and insult another human being with a racial slur? Was he given this twisted sense of entitlement from parents? Was it out of a sense of insecurity and a desire to bolster his own sense of self-worth? And were those men at the restaurant reflective of an older, more dangerous version of PC?"

The young men talked about the "good life" enjoyed across the tracks—knowing in their minds that it was promoted and sometimes enforced by the people they called "the Phillips posse." They knew who held the keys to the local economy, and that those people were effectively locking Blacks out of it. So when a coach got reassigned, an athletic director got fired, or a suspicious visitor looked in on practice, there was nothing unusual about it. It was business as usual, and the business was Phillips.

Back outside the eye-wall, the wind was whipping up—and it wasn't all about race. The Vietnam war was heating up, and protests abounded. The famous Woodstock Rock Festival was still two years away, and mass killings on the Kent State campus in Ohio came three years later. But closer to home, Bartlesville would experience firsthand, before the season ended, the death in Vietnam of one of its local heroes. Army First Lieutenant Harold Winget, a member of one the town's pioneering sports families, was reported killed in action on February 3, 1967, less than two months before his twenty-fifth birthday.

But while thousands of young men like Harold were fighting an unpopular war, there remained calm in the eye of the storm. For the Peterson family and hundreds like them, life went on as usual. David (Petey) still delivered newspapers and knocked on doors to collect the monthly payments—even during basketball season. He still attended church on Sunday and the Methodist Youth Fellowship in the evening. His family back yard played host to neighborhood sports contests, except when the cold weather forced them to the garage for table tennis games.

Of the team's white players, there were few close bonds off the court with the notable exceptions of Moose and Boody. Bob Larson and Pat Sears were free spirits—sort of "pre-Woodstock" guys without the protests. Together with their close friend Marty Lowe, the guys had often looked for ways to get in trouble. It was generally innocent mischief— teenagers having fun together—-and it even involved a musical group. Together they formed a band they called "Boody and the Batmen." By their own admission, they were no match for Scott Martin's group, "The Acemen," but life to them was about having fun. And they succeeded!

Life remained good at the Martins' house, too. They were a popular Bartlesville family—a picture of success in business and sports. Scott, as the most conspicuous junior on the team, didn't have a social relationship with the seniors. They were all friends, of course, stemming from their playing days at the Boys Club, but Scott's circle of close friends were his classmates, tennis buddies, and members of his band.

So, seemingly oblivious to the storm around them, life was good for the Wildcat basketball team. There was, however, a notable exception: Coach Sid Burton. Sid professes today to have not been consumed by the storm, but conversations with him reveal much of what he thought.

He had decided before the season that it would be his last. He considered that it was only a matter of time before he would be criticized for having too many Black players in his lineup, or that he was giving Moody or Eagle too much playing time. Perhaps it was subconscious, but Sid was waiting for the storm to make landfall, and he planned to evacuate at the right time. The classroom and the court gave him a life raft.

Meanwhile, his classes required study and preparation, exams needed to be graded, and he had a promising basketball team full of players he loved. It was little wonder that he didn't notice Denny Price.

It was also no surprise that Price's brief visit to College High didn't penetrate the wall of the storm. He was a great guy—unimposing— much the same size as the high school players, and one that many wouldn't recognize in street clothes. So when Boody and Moose took it upon themselves to organize a resistance movement, it was met with a degree of indifference. "Why should I care?" thought some of them. Had they all played football and experienced that turmoil, their reaction might have been different. "What can we do about it anyway?" asked others, not necessarily out loud. It's even curious to think why Swede Larson and G.O. Sears, fathers of the two players, would stick their necks out to stand up to Phillips. "Over what? Someone wants to help?" Those two career Phillips employees, like former coach Burl Stidham, simply wanted to do right by their boys. It's no wonder that getting an accurate, agreed upon account of the events surrounding the letter is so difficult. Some don't remember signing it—others don't recall meeting to discuss it. The explanation is offered by Boody: it was done quickly, "no muss, no fuss." Inside the eye-wall, the winds were calm and everyone wanted it to stay that way.

Much like the gymnasium walls resisted the winter wind, in that pre-Nike, pre-Under Armor era, the sounds of bouncing balls and squeaking Converses drowned out the figurative sound of the storm outside. Two major hurdles were behind them—at least for the time being. A third—the season—remained as the eye of the storm passed and the final blasts of wind approached.

PART 2

BIG HEART
IN A
SMALL TEAM

CHAPTER 17

EVERYONE BACK TO WORK

Paul Geymann headed back to the office, and the players responded to Sid's whistle by gathering around him. They had seen the last of Phillips' interference and Sid was none the wiser. Quietly, they had saved him from a headache he didn't need. It was time to think about basketball.

As Sid began drilling his disciples, similar practices were occurring all over the state. 1966 marked a change in the way Oklahoma high schools were classified for athletic competition. Until then, the highest tier had been called Class AA. To provide balance and more equitable competition, the Oklahoma Secondary School Activities Association approved a reclassification of the member schools, creating a new division of the state's thirty-two largest high schools and calling it Class AAA. The previous year's boys' basketball champions had been Tulsa Webster in Class AA, Oklahoma City Northeast in Class A, Wagoner in Class B, and Arcadia in Class C.

Two of the most heralded programs in the state leading into the 1966-67 season were Oklahoma City schools. The Northeast Vikings, upgraded from Class A to AA after winning the last championship, enjoyed a strong statewide following, with many backers claiming they could beat anyone—regardless of classification. One team stood out among all others, though—the Douglass Trojans, a star-studded AAA team coached by former Harlem Globetrotter Lawrence Cudjoe.

If the Price family was considered the "First Family of Oklahoma Basketball," another case could be made for the Cudjoes, led by twin brothers Lawrence and Lance. They were respected by knowledgeable Oklahomans of all races, but were held in particularly high esteem by the Black population. In addition to their basketball heritage, the Cudjoe family members were descendants of Black Seminoles, who fled Florida for Oklahoma in the 1830s. The brothers became known as skilled backcourt players at Booker T. Washington High School in Seminole, and gained wider fame at Langston University and with the Harlem Globetrotters. At both levels, the 5'5" twins showcased their ball-handling skill on teams that also featured the legendary Marques Haynes.

Lawrence Cudjoe first coached at Pawnee Dunbar High School before moving to Douglass, and he was in his second decade with the Trojans when the 1966 fall practices began. A perennial championship contender, this Douglass team had a tall lineup—one that figured to have everyone looking up to them, whether on the court or in the state rankings.

Kendal Cudjoe, who followed in his father's footsteps

Located one hundred fifty miles northeast of the state capital, the College High School Wildcats of Bartlesville were grouped in a competitive Class AAA conference, the Oklahoma-7, with four Tulsa schools (Rogers, Central, Hale, and Edison) plus Muskogee and Ponca City. Geographically, the league was "Tulsa-centric." There were numerous additional high schools in Tulsa, a couple of which were on the Wildcats' schedule, but Central, Edison, Hale, and Rogers were traditional rivals of College High. Bartlesville is located less than fifty miles north of Tulsa, while Muskogee is about fifty miles southeast and Ponca City some ninety miles northwest of Oklahoma's second largest city.

OKLAHOMA SEVEN (O-7) CONFERENCE

Bartlesville College High
Muskogee Central
Ponca City
Tulsa Central
Tulsa Edison
Tulsa Nathan Hale
Tulsa Will Rogers

In a poll of the league's coaches, the Edison Eagles were pre-season favorites to lead the conference, followed closely by College High and the Rogers Ropers. Bartlesville's team had completed the previous season tied for third in the league with a six and six conference record, and twelve wins and ten losses overall. The Wildcats had one glaring weakness—size—but they were respected for their experience and depth.

Sid Burton wasn't thinking about OC Douglass or any other team in the final week of November. A stickler for conditioning and preparation, Sid was working his team hard. They ran up and down the court, then up and down the bleachers, always to the sound of his whistle. They worked on fundamentals, especially passing, rebounding, and defending, but never overlooking how to complete layups and free throws. The guys were in great shape, which suited Sid to a tee. His game plans would involve a lot of running—fast breaks, full-court presses, and a tight man-to-man defense. By mid-week he had settled on his top five. Martin, Sears, and Jackson had just finished a tough four months of football and their legs were working into "basketball shape." Guery was on the court every day and night, and Peterson had played tennis during the summer and increased his leg strength through miles of bicycling. Of those, only Guery stood over 5'11", and only by a little over an inch. In addition to those five, Sid had a strong cast of other players with exceptional work habits—all of whom wanted to play. He planned to round out the first week's roster with seniors Mike Louis and Bob Larson, and juniors Steve Hale, Larry Houchin, Jack Brown, Mike Dershem, Jim Bailey, and Jim Powell. Don Wilber and Richard Edgar earned positions as student managers.

Everyone loved Sid and wanted to be part of the team. The school's pep squad, "The Peppers," and the cheerleaders were shaping up their indoor routines. No one held great expectations—they were just thrilled that the season was about to begin in a basketball-happy town and state.

Realignment, reclassification, reorganization—whatever it was called—was of no interest as the Cats polished up their practice routine. The team, via Paul Geymann, had quietly but firmly stood up to outside influence from one of the largest companies in America. Many of the players had little idea what had happened and most didn't care. Their coach had just as quietly put behind him the shadow of racism. At home with his wife, he had committed to coach one more season—but only one. He would stay with his team, live with the possibility of further obstruction, but move on when the school year ended. There was genuine love and loyalty connecting everyone on the team. Whites, Blacks, and a sole Native American would take the court and stand as one—just as they had all their lives.

Lawrence Cudjoe would finish his career as head coach at Langston University, and Lance coached at Mount St. Mary High School before becoming an administrator in the Oklahoma City school system. Each of the Cudjoe twins produced a pair of sons who followed in their fathers' footsteps. Kyle and Kendal, sons of Lawrence, have vivid memories of watching their father's Douglass teams, particularly the star-studded team of the 1966-67 season, which Kendal remembers as his dad's greatest team. Not to be outdone by his father's record, Kendal would later become the Douglass coach and lead his team to multiple state championships. Among the most memorable games, at least to Oklahoma high school fans, was the 2017 AAA state championship game when Douglass defeated Star Spencer High School, also of Oklahoma City, 62-56. Star Spencer was coached by Kendal's cousin, Lance Cudjoe, Jr. Lance's brother Patrick would become the boys' coach at Oklahoma City John Marshall, leading them to over four hundred wins and a state championship, and Kendal would later move to Classen School of Advanced Studies (SAS) High School.

These and many other accomplishments of the Cudjoe family continue to this day, but those who know the state's basketball history will long remember that the rich high school legacy of the Cudjoe family began in earnest with Lawrence and the Douglass Trojans.

Sources: "The Oklahoman," published February 20, 2002, author Bob Colon "CapitolBeatOK" March 11, 2017, Patrick B. McGuigan

CHAPTER 18

SEASON TIPOFF

With football season three weeks behind them, and the coaching distractions nearly forgotten, December brought both a change in the weather and exciting challenges to the Wildcats. They would eventually focus on a difficult Oklahoma-7 (O-7) Conference schedule, but their early games featured tough non-conference foes from all over northeast Oklahoma and beyond. There were teams from smaller towns like Miami, Pryor, and Vinita, but also from Tulsa schools McLain, Kelly, Hale, and Cascia Hall. Even a team from Ft. Smith, Arkansas, would journey to one of the Tulsa tournaments.

In the Wildcats' case, under Coach Sid Burton, there was no looking ahead, at least not beyond the next game on the schedule. There was no swagger, no star quality, no great record from previous seasons, and certainly no size! What the players had was held deep inside of them—it was "togetherness," an ability to share both the basketball and the glory, and the confidence gained from years of being winners. Individually or together, they had won championships in tennis, Little League baseball, junior high football, and yes—in basketball as kids in the state AAU tournament.

In addition, the team had leadership. On the court they relied on four returning starters, three of whom were seniors. The fourth, Scott Martin, took second to no one in the leadership category, having just completed a season as the football team's starting quarterback. David Peterson was the least experienced of the group, but would quickly dispel any anxiety about his leadership capability. On the bench, Sid Burton seemed to be the perfect match for the boys on the court, and for the capable cast of reserves at his side. He also had a highly competent assistant in Don Calvert, whose duties included coaching the B Team and coordinating scouting of future opponents.

Sid's demeanor was exemplary. Even today his players remember that he never berated or belittled them, seldom even raised his voice, and always made them feel important. They didn't fear making mistakes, knowing that only lack of hustle would get them in Sid's doghouse. What did being in his doghouse mean? Running and more running, frequently up and down the fieldhouse steps, and usually to the tune of Sid's famous whistle. Those disciplinary measures led to his nickname, "Coach Sid Whistle Drills." In games, no matter the score, Sid remained composed. He didn't confront or chastise officials, and he never embarrassed a player over a mistake.

With that type of leadership, the undersized College High School Wildcats embarked confidently but quietly on the 1966-67 season.

The inaugural game was in front of a friendly home crowd in the College High gym, hosting an overmatched Miami team. Ernest Guery and Pat Sears, known and loved as Moody and Boody, led the scoring with sixteen and fifteen points, respectively. The reserves saw a lot of action, with ten players scoring. Steve Hale led the bench in scoring with ten points, and the Cats dumped in ten of twelve free throw attempts.

That initial game was played on Friday, December 2, and the team's next start wasn't scheduled until the following Thursday. Although the season was extremely young, the break was timely. The coming weekend featured a tournament hosted by Tulsa McLain, with three games on three successive nights. Although Bartlesville and Tulsa were separated by only fifty miles or so, the schedule required the team to climb into their big yellow bus for the hour-long trip before and after each of the three games. Preparing for that tournament was one of Sid's first big challenges of the season.

Despite their easy win over Miami, Sid and his team knew they hadn't been tested. The starters played hard, but barely broke a sweat. Their confidence was up, but they knew they needed to work. Practices were demanding with Sid insisting on hustle. He preached "pass and cut," "move the ball," "don't slow it down," and "pass and pick." The sound of his whistle might mean "take a break," or it could mean "run some sprints." There was no time to celebrate their season's opener. Three games awaited them in Tulsa.

Northeast Oklahoma enjoyed unseasonably warm days that first full week in December. Daily highs averaged in the mid to low seventies from Monday through Thursday, but Oklahomans aren't fooled by days like that. Nearly a half-inch of rain fell on College High Thursday morning, part of a cold front that would bring a drastic change during the tournament. After a high of seventy-six on Thursday, the local weather observers would record a low of fifteen degrees on Saturday.

Fortunately, basketball is an indoor sport, and the temperature inside the Tulsa McLain High School gym would remain steady—and warm. The eight teams who came to play would ensure that no one was concerned with the weather outside. No team played at a higher tempo than the boys from Bartlesville. They ran, passed, cut, and defended with high energy, demonstrating depth, balance, and desire. In the opening game on Thursday, the Cats demonstrated all those qualities, trouncing the Comets of Tulsa's Bishop Kelley High School, 62-27. David Peterson, starting for only the second time in his career, led the scoring with twelve points while playing only about half the game. Moody Guery added ten of his own, and Steve Hale, for the second straight game, had ten points off the bench. The Wildcats' man-to-man defense was stifling, holding the Comets to three points in the first quarter, and charging to a 31-12 halftime lead.

The team from the relatively small town of Pryor had little trouble with Sapulpa, a team from the Tulsa suburbs, on Thursday night, but failed to mount much of a charge on the tournament's second night. Clearly lacking the speed and cohesiveness of the Wildcat lineup, Pryor fell to Bartlesville, 87-39. Once again able to use his talented reserves, Sid watched happily as Scott Martin scored seventeen points, Moody and Boody added fourteen each, and Ernie "Eagle" Jackson soared high to add ten. The players had a relaxing bus trip home—grateful for the margins of victory that permitted starters to rest and reserves to contribute in a big way to both wins.

	FG	FT	TOTAL POINTS
Guery	7	0	14
Sears	6	2	14
Martin	6	5	17
Peterson	2	1	5
Jackson	3	4	10
Louis	4	0	8
Larson	1	1	3
Hale	1	2	4
Brown	2	0	4
Dershem	1	0	2
Houchin	2	0	4
Bailey	0	0	0
Powell	1	0	2
Total	**36**	**15**	**87**

FINAL SCORE: **Bartlesville 87, Pryor 39**

By the time they got back on the bus Saturday, everyone could feel the penetrating stabs of the winter wind. Nevertheless, the Cats were upbeat, confident, and happy to be playing in a tournament championship game. Their opponent would be O-7 Conference rival Tulsa Central, a team that had been coached the previous seven seasons by Eddie Sutton, a man who would go on to win more than 800 games in his Hall-of-Fame college coaching career. The game was the first of at least three season matchups scheduled between the two schools.

Perhaps fatigue set in that evening, the result of three games in fifty hours, as the Central Braves played a slow-tempo game for the first half. They pressed the Wildcats more after the halftime break, but Bartlesville's skilled ball handling prevailed and the team survived to win the championship, 54-47. Scott Martin and Ernest Guery led the team in scoring with sixteen points apiece, and both were named to the all-tournament team.

	FG	FT	TOTAL POINTS
Guery	7	2	16
Sears	1	0	2
Martin	5	6	16
Peterson	4	1	9
Jackson	2	3	7
Louis	1	0	2
Hale	1	0	2
Total	21	12	54

HALFTIME: **Bartlesville 24, Central 16**

FINAL SCORE: **Bartlesville 54, Central 47**

Winning a tournament championship was a first for all of the players at the high school level, and they joyously returned to school with a large trophy, taking pleasure in gathering Monday morning to present it to school principal John Haley. Their celebration was short-lived, however, as two more games awaited them that week, the first one falling on Tuesday. Such is the life of high school basketball players—usually playing games on Tuesdays and Fridays while practicing the other three days. In a way, that prepares them for college athletics by teaching them how to balance athletics with the demands of the classroom. All of the players—starters and reserves—aspired to attend college, and most of them expected to continue as student-athletes. Sid, too, had classroom responsibilities, and his American History students never observed any difference in the energy level he brought to the classroom, regardless of the basketball schedule.

The night after delivering the McLain Tournament trophy to school, Sid and the boys returned to non-conference action with a home game against Vinita. Another school comparable in size to Miami and Pryor, the Hornets were decidedly outmatched in their visit to College High, resulting in a lopsided win for the home team. The Wildcats nearly doubled Vinita's scoring, 69-35. Once again the depth and balance were evident, with Martin scoring seventeen points, followed by Moody and Boody with fourteen each. Five games into the season, the undefeated Wildcats had averaged 67.6 points per game while holding the opposition to an average of just thirty-eight. Things were beginning to click—and just in time, for the conference opener versus Muskogee was just three days away.

McLain Tourney action

CHAPTER 19

COUNTDOWN TO CHRISTMAS

As competition with league opponents loomed, so did the usually friendly, traditional rivalries of teams from Bartlesville and Muskogee. There were of course the four Tulsa schools to be reckoned with, but those teams were far from dominant. The schools from Ponca City, Bartlesville, and Muskogee had long been rivals of the Tulsa teams, and each had a rich legacy of athletic competition. Muskogee Central High School, for example, had been regarded as a "football factory" in the early to mid-fifties, providing a pipeline of future stars to Bud Wilkinson at the University of Oklahoma. Names like Eddie Crowder, the Burris brothers (Buddy, Kurt, Bob, Lynn, Lyle, and Don), Bo Bollinger, and Max Boydston were all household names when Wilkinson assembled some of the greatest college teams in the country. So even with the dawn of another basketball season, Muskogee folks maintained their pride in football.

To reach Bartlesville, the bus carrying the Roughers' basketball team had to skirt Tulsa on a trip that took about two hours. The roads were clear, the weather mild for mid-December with the temperature forecast to remain above freezing until long after the game. The players arrived an hour prior to the game, donned their visiting uniforms, and took the court for pregame drills. Sadly for the Roughers, no amount of preparation could have made their conference opener successful.

The game itself was a mismatch from the beginning. Before it ended, Sid Burton used all of his players, with ten scoring. The reserves played the entire fourth quarter, with Steve Hale leading the bench in scoring. For the third time in the first six games, the hard-working junior dropped in ten points on three for five shooting. Mike Louis, Jim Bailey, Mike Dershem, and Bob Larson added two points each, prompting Sid's postgame comment, "After all, that's what these kids are looking forward to. If you don't let them play, they soon lose interest in the club."

	FG	FT	TOTAL POINTS
Guery	4-9	1-1	9
Sears	3-6	3-5	9
Martin	3-7	6-8	12
Peterson	3-4	5-6	11
Jackson	2-2	3-5	7
Louis	1-2	0-0	2
Hale	3-5	4-5	10
Larson	2-5	0-0	4
Bailey	1-3	0-0	2
Dershem	0-1	2-2	2
Brown	0-1	0-0	0
Houchin	0-3	0-0	0
Total	**22-48**	**24-34**	**68**

HALFTIME: **Bartlesville 34, Muskogee 26**
FINAL SCORE: **Bartlesville 68, Muskogee 48**

Only the coming Christmas break could cause anyone to lose interest, but Sid and his team knew they had one more test awaiting them. Fortunately, the Cats were healthy and well-rested following their easy win over Muskogee, because the final opponent in 1966 would be the league's preseason favorites, the Edison Eagles. Holiday parties, girlfriends, and Santa Claus would have to wait.

Sid's focus on preparation for the trip to Tulsa remained steady. His whistle was busy, and the players responded with enthusiasm. He stressed getting up the court quickly, moving the ball crisply, and always maintaining good spacing. With their usual height disadvantage, blocking out for rebounds was essential. All of the starters did their part in rebounding, but "the Eagle," Ernie Jackson could outjump bigger men, and Moody Guery could always find perfect positioning. Lack of height never seemed to be a problem for Sid and the boys. Neither was overconfidence.

By Wednesday, December 21, the team was ready and eager as each player took his seat on the "Yellow Dog" for the hour-long trip to Tulsa. The trip passed so quickly that sack lunches had to wait until the trip home—frequently a sore point for Boody. He recalled being told by Sid on a previous trip that "A hungry tiger hunts best," only to respond, "Yes, Sid, but a tiger dead from starvation doesn't hunt at all." Discussion completed, the Cats waited until after the game to eat.

> *Scott Martin described the ham and cheese sandwiches in the brown bags as "mostly bread," but conceded that the apples and chips were normally "okay."*

Following the game between the two schools' B teams, in a packed gym with a raucous Edison crowd, the Wildcats of College High School served notice that the O-7 Conference race would be a good one, defeating the favored Eagles, 53-49. The contest was close throughout, with the visiting Cats leading by four at the half. David Peterson, who had hit a remarkable twenty of twenty-four field goals in prior games, was held to one of six shooting by the Eagles. He was picked up, however, by the lone junior starter, Scott Martin. Sport enjoyed his finest performance of the young season, hitting an impressive array of jumpers and drives. Martin accounted for nearly half of the team's points with twenty-six, including a perfect ten for ten from the free throw line.

	FG	FT	TOTAL POINTS
Guery	6	1-3	13
Sears	4	1-3	9
Martin	8	10-10	26
Peterson	1	2-3	4
Jackson	0	1-1	1
Louis	0	0-1	0
Hale	0	0-0	0
Total	**19**	**15-21**	**53**

HALFTIME: **Bartlesville 29, Edison 25**

FINAL SCORE: **Bartlesville 53, Edison 49**

Tulsa Tribune reporter Bob Cobb quoted Sid in the following day's paper: "I've already had a pretty good present. That makes for a good vacation. This race hasn't started. It's going to be like it's always been… nip and tuck. The winner may lose three games and still take the title. There are no real weak sisters this year."

CHAPTER 20

BUMPS IN THE ROAD

Schools in northeast Oklahoma adjourned for the Christmas recess in the midst of an early winter snowstorm. It was Friday, December 23, when six inches of the white powder created a blanket across the region. The impact on Sid and the boys was minimal, as all of them lived within four miles of the school. Those were the days before colleges began recruiting athletes in middle schools—a practice that led to high schools also recruiting and developing the questionable practices of bringing youngsters from distant areas to their schools. For the Wildcats, commuting wasn't an issue—Scott Martin could walk across the street and the others could either drive themselves or carpool. Besides, Christmas was only two days away, as was the predicted melting, and the following week would be filled with social activities. For the seventeen- and eighteen-year-olds, it was a welcome break from basketball's daily grind, although each of them would receive a Christmas card signed "Coach Sid Whistle Drills."

GREETINGS

AND GOOD WISHES

FOR CHRISTMAS AND THE COMING YEAR

COACH SID WHISTLE-DRILLS

Sid's Christmas card

With Christmas and New Year's both falling on Sundays, the holiday break was a short one—just the week between them. The heavy snow that fell on the 23rd still lingered a week later, with drifts created by snow plows still over a foot deep in the College High parking lot. They had been preserved by bitterly cold temperatures, even by Oklahoma standards, one night falling to five below zero. Sid felt like the cold weather and short break justified a full week off, so the players returned on the second day of 1967 with fresh legs—eager for a game the following night.

Although December had been a good month, the team's return to practice was marked, not by cockiness, but by determination and a key characteristic of the team—grit. The players mirrored their coach's calm, serious disposition. There was no talk of winning championships—only of preparing for the next opponent.

When lessons were needed, Sid had his unique way of teaching them, as players on all of his teams knew. For example, Bobby Jones was a pitcher on Sid's College High baseball team from 1960 to '62. The hard-throwing right hander was one of the team's true stars, so good that he was named most valuable player on the Wildcats' roster his senior year. For Jones, though, receiving the award wasn't important enough personally for him to attend the end-of-season banquet. Still, decades later he recalled Sid finding him at school the next day and handing him the award. The presentation was made silently, without the coach saying a word. Jones remembers that moment as a lesson. In typical Sid fashion, no words were necessary so none were spoken. Jones knew that Sid was disappointed and that was enough.

The basketball team that reconvened in early 1967 knew that about Sid, too. Just a look from him was often enough to correct a mistake. If lack of hustle was a factor, Sid would hold his whistle near his ear—and quietly ask "what do I hear?" The suggestion of a looming whistle drill was reason enough to work a little harder. Sid could be tough if needed. His version of the proverbial "woodshed" was a storage closet in the hallway outside the gym—underneath the rows of wooden benches used by spectators. That closet had become a too familiar meeting place the previous season for two of Sid's favorite whipping boys, Pat (Boody) Sears and Bob (Moose) Larson. The most serious occurrences in that room weren't actual whippings, just heart-to-heart talks ranging from girlfriend problems to teenage shenanigans. It wasn't that they went there frequently, but more than once was too many, and Moose and Boody eventually straightened up. Their most serious problem in Sid's eyes was their tendency to have a little too much fun, sometimes at the coach's expense. Midway through their senior year, both had grown up considerably—and just in time!

The first Tuesday of the new year meant a seventy-mile trip west to Ponca City for a game against the "other" Wildcats. The battle for first place in the O-7 Conference matched the small College High team against a talented squad with a pair of 6'4" front court players in Bobby Jack and Gerald Young. Perhaps feeling a little rusty from the holidays, both teams were ragged, and earned more than their normal fouls and turnovers. Still, the see-saw game provided plenty of excitement with the Poncans rallying to outscore the visitors by five points in the fourth quarter to win, 64-62. Boody Sears enjoyed a good first quarter and Sport Martin erupted for fifteen second-half points. Moody Guery, despite limited time in the second and third quarters, was second in scoring, with seventeen to Martin's twenty. The difference in the game, however, boiled down to free throw performance, with Ponca City sinking twenty-two of thirty-two, while the Bartians were only sixteen of twenty-eight. Sid's reaction? According to the next day's *Bartlesville Examiner-Enterprise*, he said, "Our inability to hit our short shots and their ability to hit the long ones beat us. But, I don't think this game will hurt the team morale. If anything, it'll help…"

Sid was right, as usual. His team responded to their first loss of the season by practicing Wednesday and Thursday in businesslike fashion, taking Sid's advice and quickly shaking off Tuesday's defeat. At that point, their modest expectations for the season were an asset. Since no one had even dreamed of going undefeated, they were far from crushed over losing their first game. As always, the focus was on the next opponent. So "pass and cut," "pass and screen," "move the ball," and "hustle down the court" could be heard over and over. Sid never tired of encouraging his players, both starters and reserves, and the players never seemed to tire of hearing him. They were responsive and determined—their second tournament of the season was about to begin.

CHAPTER 21

"TAKE ME BACK TO TULSA"

The words of the legendary Bob Wills rang true for the Wildcats. It was time to climb on the bus and make the trip down U.S. 75 once again. The miles on the mostly straight road passed quickly. Moose led the customary "SALUTE" passing the Moose Lodge, Ernie studied, some napped briefly, and they soon found themselves on the Tulsa outskirts.

Oral Roberts University was still new to Tulsa that winter. Ground had been broken in 1962, but the college didn't officially open until 1965. It was still too early in the young school's life to boast a big gymnasium, but not too soon to host an invitational basketball tournament. So, in a rather small facility on the school's new south Tulsa campus, four high school teams met on the first weekend of 1967. Boody Sears recalls that the gym was similar in size to the College High field house, but with fewer seats.

Only four teams were invited to play at ORU that weekend; in addition to the Wildcats, the field included the Tulsa Hale Rangers and teams from Ft. Smith and Morrilton, Arkansas. In Friday night action, Hale had little trouble with Morrilton while the Cats advanced to the final game by handing Ft. Smith Southside a 75-65 loss. Once again displaying depth and balance, nine Bartlesville players scored, led by Martin and Guery with sixteen points each.

As with all of their games, the team returned home on the "Yellow Dog" after the game, only to return less than twenty hours later. The weather was much like winter everywhere—unpredictable! Friday had been unseasonably warm with the temperature reaching sixty-three during the trip to Tulsa. Saturday, though, with the heater on the bus barely working, the players could frequently see their breath. The official high was thirty-four degrees, but it seemed much colder on the creaky old bus.

A warm gym awaited them when they disembarked for their game with Hale, a team they were scheduled to play twice more in conference competition in the next ten days. It was important to Sid to "set the tone," letting everyone in Tulsa know that his team could compete. Edison and Central had learned that in December, but Hale and Rogers lurked, as did a non-conference Tulsa school, Cascia Hall. Tulsa players and fans, as well as their press corps, wanted to see if the Wildcats were for real.

The answer became more apparent, if not totally convincing, Saturday night at ORU. In the small but packed gym, the undersized Cats put on another display of solid all-around team ability, outscoring Tulsa Hale 65-54. Led by David Peterson's eighteen points and fifteen apiece from Martin and Guery, the Cats ran their season record to nine and one, earning their second new tournament trophy for the glass case near the school office.

Two wins on successive nights gave Sid and his team an emotional lift. Not that they were particularly down after the loss to Ponca City, but the cold, dreary days of an Oklahoma winter were upon them. Days were short, exams were imminent, and basketball was their only escape. Balancing studies with practices was always difficult, but this time it was more important than ever. All of the players planned to attend college, and most were in the process of finishing their applications. They needed to show solid grades on the applications. Sid, a teacher first and then a coach, made sure his players shared his priorities. Classroom attendance was never an issue for athletes at College High.

A rematch with Tulsa Hale was first up after the ORU tournament. Back-to-back games versus the same team can lead to overconfidence, and Sid was determined to avoid that. The players were relaxed at Monday's practice, but Sid emphasized fundamentals. He stressed crisp ball movement, bounce passes when appropriate, keeping their heads up, looking ahead on fast breaks, and always playing tough defense. He felt they were ready for Hale once again by the time they headed for the showers.

If the Hale Rangers expected any letdown from the visiting Wildcats, they were sadly disappointed. In a flashy show of "run and gun," the shorter, quicker Bartians made it "run and fun." With a comfortable lead throughout most of the game, Sid gave the reserves a chance to show their ability. The result was a 64-47 rout of the Rangers, with twelve Cats scoring. Again it was balanced, with Moody, Boody, Sport, and Eagle each scoring from ten to twelve points, and seven of the eight reserves adding to the total. The fun extended well into the trip back to Bartlesville!

Halfway through the season, the Wildcats had recorded ten wins and one loss and had extremely balanced statistics. They led the O-7 Conference in both offense and defense, and the players' scoring was well distributed. The lone junior starter, Martin led with a 13.8 average, followed by Guery at 13.1. Peterson averaged 9.6, Sears 8.7, Jackson 7.7, and reserve Steve Hale added 4.8 per game. They had outscored their opponents by an average of nineteen points, but still trailed Tulsa Rogers in the conference race.

Three days later, on Friday the 13th, the team boarded the bus once again for a trip to Tulsa. The players paid little attention to the sights outside, preferring to nap, read, or tell jokes. They were loose and relaxed, but far from cocky. They knew Tulsa Central would be ready and especially eager to avenge their tournament loss to the Cats in December. And this time, Central would have the home court advantage, and what an advantage it was! The court had almost no space between one of its sidelines and a high, solid wall, with seats above it. Marty Lowe recalls playing there and barely having room for his size nine shoes to fit out of bounds when passing the ball into play. "Had I worn a size ten," Marty says, "my toes would have been on the line." David Peterson remembers all too vividly the play that night when Jim Benien, a shot put and discus standout, delivered a cross-body block that pinned the much smaller Petey against the wall. The resulting free throws were shot by Steve Hale, Peterson's replacement for the remaining two and a half quarters. The Cats were undeterred by Central's physicality and Moody Guery led the scoring parade with fourteen points. Sid and the boys left Benien and his wrecking crew behind with a 48-36 victory, once again earning an enjoyable ride back up Highway 75.

CHAPTER 22

THREE'S A CHARM

It's often said, particularly with conference rivals, that beating the same team twice in a season is hard. Doing it three times is next to impossible. That was the challenge facing the Wildcats as they prepared on Monday for the next day's game against Tulsa's Nathan Hale High School Rangers. Having defeated them on Saturday the 7th and Tuesday the 10th, the Cats would finally get to play them at home on the 17th. Under blue skies and seasonable temperatures outside, Sid pushed the boys inside the gym to avoid overconfidence. Petey remembers the emphasis their coach placed on fastbreak execution. Whether two-on-one or three-on-two, Sid was a stickler for proper spacing and passes that led the receiver perfectly. No-look and bounce passes, as well as ball fakes, were all on the menu, and the players wanted perfection as much as Sid did. All of them, reserves included, were knowledgeable and skilled in the art of ball handling. Above all, they followed the mantra of "stay alert—you never know when the ball may come to you." As the Cats would learn in coming weeks, truer words were never spoken.

The Rangers were a proud group, stung by two recent losses to College High and determined to not lose again. Alas, it happened again, but not without drama. The Cats withstood an unusually cold shooting night which led to a 42-30 deficit late in the third quarter. Their never-say-die attitude was exemplified by the tenacious play of reserve Moose Larson, whose defense gave them the chance they needed. The Wildcats missed thirty of their fifty field goal attempts while Hale was shooting fifty percent, but Larson and his teammates forced enough mistakes to limit their rivals to only thirty-eight shots. That allowed the home team to climb back into it, finally tying the game at 52 with under a minute left. Coach Burton chose to hold the ball for a late shot, letting his capable point guard, Martin, work the clock down. With Hale dropping back, Sport couldn't find the layup he hoped for, and dished the ball to Sears with time running out. Boody's twenty-foot jumper sealed the victory, the crowd exploded, and Boody was mobbed and carried off the court. The magical season continued!

Crunch time in the O-7 Conference was upon them, and also for the Ropers of Tulsa Rogers, the conference leaders as their first season matchup drew near. The Will Rogers team remained undefeated in league play and had shown no weaknesses through the first seven weeks of the season. Their home game versus Bartlesville on January 20 would be decisive in the race for supremacy. Sid and his team knew it, and their practices on Wednesday and Thursday were key in preparing for the all-important upcoming game. As always, the team remained focused on the next game, never mentioning or even dreaming of a conference championship. Led and inspired by their coach, the players were locked on to one goal—winning Friday's game. Bodies began to ache a little and there were some minor foot blisters. But Petey's injury in the Central game had mended quickly and the team enjoyed all-around good health. They were a tremendously conditioned group and ready to hit the road once again.

The athleticism and conditioning of Petey and his teammates were never more important than late in the game against Rogers. Trailing down the stretch for the second time in four days, the Cats were again propelled back into contention by the defense of Moose Larson. Mike Louis, another steady reserve, ignored a boisterous student section and scored four key points in overtime to give the visitors a hard-earned victory, 58-57. The home court would never look better.

Home it would be, four days later, when the Edison Eagles rode into town, seeking revenge for their narrow December loss. Edison coach Larry Rentfro was disappointed in his team's three conference losses, but still wanted a say in the season's final standings. As the preseason favorites, he knew his team could beat anyone on a given night. Besides, he had seen the ups and downs of the Wildcats, commenting that they "played like a college team against us," but like just another high school team against Central. He expressed surprise that a Tulsa newspaper poll ranked the Bartlesville team as number two in the state. The Wildcats, meanwhile, seemed oblivious to the rankings. They simply had another game to win, and Edison was the opponent.

Unfortunately for the Eagles, the College High court didn't make life any easier for them. The red-hot Wildcats put their shooting woes behind them and connected on forty-seven percent of their field goal attempts. Moody Guery led the attack with twenty points, followed by David Peterson with fifteen, Boody Sears with fourteen, and junior Scott Martin with thirteen. The 71-59 victory, coupled with Tulsa Rogers' 53-48 win over Ponca City, left the Wildcats up by a half-game over Rogers in the tight conference race. The only tense moment for the Bartlesville faithful was when crowd-favorite Ernie Jackson seemed to hobble off the court with an ankle or knee injury.

0-7 Conference Standings

| | Conference Games | | All Games | |
	WIN	LOSS	WIN	LOSS
Bartlesville	7	1	14	1
Rogers	6	1	12	2
Ponca City	6	2	8	3
Central	2	4	7	7
Edison	2	4	7	7
Muskogee	2	6	5	8
Hale	0	7	3	12

Six straight games against Tulsa schools—six consecutive wins. What could be better? With three weeks left in the season, Bartlesville's conference record was seven and one, compared to six and one for the Ropers. Sid was understandably happy after the game, but in his reserved fashion he said only that improved rebounding and fast-break execution led to their seventh consecutive win. There was still a lot of work to be done, as well as needing to deal with an injury.

CHAPTER 23

THE STRETCH RUN

With three weeks left until the playoffs, everyone except Sid and his players was starting to sense big things for the Wildcats. The team had begun to appear near the top of state AAA rankings, never far behind everyone's top-rated team, Oklahoma City Douglass. The Trojans, led by consensus high school All-American Amos Thomas, were simply blowing every opponent away. Thomas wasn't their only star, either, as he was joined in a starting lineup where four of the five starters measured 6'3" or taller. Thomas himself stood 6'7" and possessed dazzling skills, the kind that would eventually make him a second-round NBA draft pick. As long as Douglass kept on winning—and winning big—no one, even the most avid Wildcat fans, dreamed of anyone but the Trojans dominating the other state AAA programs.

Nevertheless, high school basketball was having an effect on Bartians. The most ardent of fans had never seen anyone but their beloved 66ers play together like the Cats did that winter. They knew good basketball when they saw it. Besides, it was taking place on a fully integrated basketball team, unlike the all-white 66ers. Ernest Guery, Ernie Jackson, and Mike Louis were the products of a segregated, Black neighborhood, their families part of a distinctly disadvantaged community where they had been denied opportunities to play with the more privileged kids of Bartlesville. Never could they have played on the Phillips 33ers with Martin, Peterson, Sears, and others. It wasn't that any of the Phillips kids considered themselves privileged—lucky perhaps, but mostly it was just something they took for granted. The memories, both good and bad, were from recent years, but basketball had a way of pushing the bad ones aside, perhaps compartmentalizing them.

The season's success also helped dim the memory of Denny Price visiting that early practice, while Sid managed to temporarily shed the memory of his friend Burl's firing over a racial issue. Life was good, at least for the time being, and school spirit at College High was rising.

The final game of January was a home rematch versus Ponca City on Friday the 27th. The winter's second snow fell on Bartlesville, leaving an inch on the ground—not enough to affect the bus trip from Ponca. The "other" Wildcats desperately needed a second win over College High to remain alive in the tight conference race, and they brought all their artillery with them. That included the league's leading scorer, 6'4" Gerald Young, who was averaging nearly twenty points per game. To counter him, Sid announced that 6'3" Mike Louis would start in place of Ernie Jackson, who had sprained an ankle in the Edison game. The team had confidence in Louie, who had come up big in overtime at Rogers. Again, the lanky reserve rose to the occasion. With nine points and seven huge rebounds, Louis led his team to an easy 79-55 victory that effectively ended Ponca City's title hopes.

The game's final numbers reveal just how dominating Sid's Wildcats were. They opened the game with a 23-6 lead, hitting eight of their first eleven shots. Ponca City had only one rebound in the first quarter, and by halftime trailed 38-18. Martin led all scorers with seventeen points, and each of the other starters added at least nine—all despite limited playing time. The reserves added twenty-one points, including all of the team's fourth quarter scoring. Sid had thirteen players in uniform for the game, and even B-Team stalwart Jim Powell contributed to the scoring. Notably, Gerald Young fouled out late in the game, having grabbed only five rebounds. Ponca City returned home on snow-lined U.S. Highway 60, their hopes of a conference title gone in the dark of a moonless night.

Ponca City	FG	FT	TOTAL
Young	3	5-7	11
Orr	0	0-0	0
Dorcheus	3	2-4	8
Jones	3	4-5	10
Jack	6	4-7	16
Cook	3	3-8	9
Coates	0	1-2	1
Total	18	19-33	55

Bartlesville	FG	FT	TOTAL
Guery	5	1-2	11
Peterson	4	1-2	9
Sears	3	6-6	12
Martin	5	7-7	17
Louis	4	1-1	9
Brown	1	2-2	4
Larson	3	1-3	7
Bailey	1	0-0	2
Hale	0	0-0	0
Powell	0	1-2	1
Jackson	1	0-1	2
Dershem	0	2-2	2
Houchin	1	1-4	3
Total	28	23-32	79

HALFTIME: **Bartlesville 38, Ponca City 18**

With his ankle on the mend, Eagle took a rare weekend break for a recruiting visit to the University of Notre Dame in South Bend, Indiana. There he was met by their heaviest snowfall of the year—perhaps many years—when nearly three feet of new fallen flakes greeted him on his arrival. While the snow was deep enough to delay his return until Wednesday, it didn't prevent the students from attending classes. Those two days of visiting, dining, and attending classes with the student-athletes proved pivotal when Ernie finalized his college plans. Upon returning to Bartlesville, Ernie swore that he wouldn't return to the cold of Indiana, and had been visited by Oklahoma coach Jim Mackenzie, among others. But Ernie would long recall the close-knit student body at Notre Dame, including the way athletes bonded with their fellow students, and would ultimately follow his heart back to South Bend.

Back in Bartlesville, February's arrival brought with it a break, not only a week between games, but also two weeks before the next conference matchup. There was also Groundhog Day, when another snowfall left an inch on the ground, but it melted rapidly as temperatures rose to the sixties by Saturday. Before the snow disappeared completely, the Wildcats had another trip scheduled down Highway 75. The February 3rd matchup was with Cascia Hall, a private Catholic school located slightly southeast of downtown Tulsa. The Commandos, under young first-year coach Rick Park, were trying to turn their program around. Fifteen games into the season, they were showing progress, counting a victory over Tulsa Central among their nine wins. But everyone, even Coach Park, knew that a home win over the Wildcats would take an extraordinary effort—and perhaps a little luck.

From the opening tipoff, the effort was definitely there for the underdog Commandos. College High was back at full strength, Ernie Jackson's ankle strong again, but sluggish play enabled Cascia Hall to stay close. The Cats actually trailed the Commandos late in the third quarter, 30-29, until a late surge gave them a four-point lead at the final break. Ultimately it was Moody Guery's eighteen-point performance that shone the brightest, and led the visitors to a 55-45 win. Mike Louis was once again strong off the bench, adding ten important points for the red hot Cats.

The following Tuesday featured another non-conference game, the last for the Wildcats in their regular (non-playoff) season. The sixteen and one Cats, after a routine Monday practice, jumped on the "Yellow Dog" for a trip east on Highway 60 to Vinita. Tensions were down and spirits were up on the hour-long trip through Nowata and a wide spot in the road called Coody's Bluff. Sid's boys were more relaxed than they'd been all season, and why not? They were beginning to be recognized statewide for what they were—a really good basketball team. Not that any of that would go to their heads; they knew that it was hard work that got them near the top. All of them came from solid, unified families, and their parents had imbued in them their strong values of love and loyalty.

Critical for the Wildcats was the return of Eagle. Looking at box scores and game summaries might lead less informed fans to underestimate the importance of Ernie Jackson to the Cats' lineup. But Bartians were far from being uninformed. Basketball was a major part of the town's culture, and playing it the right way was an expectation. Ernie played it right. He was an extremely popular student, one whose easygoing nature around friends and teachers belied the tenacity he displayed in sports competition. Yet, in both football and basketball, his disposition and his ease in doing things right served to be both calming and inspiring to his teammates. Coming off an all-state football season, he adapted readily, as did Sport and Boody, to the demands of basketball. Seldom a high scorer, he was nevertheless an invaluable cog in Sid's wheel, a player who exemplified the qualities of perfect positioning, precise passing, unsurpassed leaping ability, and total selflessness. As they stepped off the bus in Vinita, the guys were glad to have Eagle back.

It took all of Eagle's effort, plus considerable help from everyone else, to subdue the much-improved Vinita Hornets, 65-54. The Wildcats were hot from the field, sinking twenty-nine of fifty-nine attempts, and shut down the inspired Hornets when it mattered most. Martin led the scoring parade with twenty-three points, followed by Jackson with twelve and the Moody/Boody combo with eleven each. The end was in sight, with only Muskogee, Central, and Rogers remaining before the state tournament.

CHAPTER 24

"On the Road Again"

Willie Nelson could have had the Wildcats in mind when he wrote one of his signature songs, because next up for the seventeen and one Wildcats was a trip to Muskogee, where the arch-rival Roughers hoped to avenge their December drubbing in Bartlesville. In the long history of the series between the two teams, seldom had there been such a disparity in records. Muskogee would defend its home court with only a four and five conference record, and eight and nine overall. Nevertheless, nothing would please the Roughers more than knocking the Wildcats out of conference contention. Tulsa Rogers traveled to Ponca City the same night, and a win for the Ropers, coupled with a College High loss, would dash the Cats' hopes of winning the championship.

One of Oklahoma's true football factories, Muskogee would be put on the national map later by country singer Merle Haggard, but the only true "Okie from Muskogee" in country music is Carrie Underwood, born there in 1983.

The Yellow Dog

Rogers took care of their end of business that night, edging the Ponca City Wildcats 49-45. They won the hard way, coming from five points down in the final minute to avoid an upset. It was slightly easier for Bartlesville, who jumped off to an early 7-0 lead and held on to win 65-57 in front of 3,000 fans in Muskogee. The Wildcats uncharacteristically committed seventeen turnovers, but offset that with strong shooting and rebounding. Scott Martin again led all scorers with twenty-two points, including a perfect ten for ten from the free throw line. Guery and Sears added seventeen and sixteen points, while Ernie Jackson grabbed a game-high fourteen rebounds. Sid was satisfied, but not ecstatic. His postgame comments were succinct and indicative of his focus: "There is only one important game for us— Tulsa Central." [*Bartlesville Examiner-Enterprise*]

The team enjoyed the weekend off, as always, but returned to practice Monday afternoon with renewed focus. The players shared their coach's intensity and his belief that only the next game really mattered. Central, frankly, wasn't a great team. The team that Eddie Sutton built was gone, just like their gifted coach. Most had graduated, leaving rookie coach Jim Howard with a determined but youthful squad. Worse yet, they would be missing Jim Benien, the villain of the most recent game versus Bartlesville, who was suffering from extreme weight loss. The Braves stood sixth in the O-7 Conference, just ahead of Tulsa Hale, and two of their twelve losses had come at the hands of the Wildcats. Despite that, they had been tough and physical in the first two games, and Sid didn't expect them to back off in the third matchup.

In Monday's drills, Sid urged the reserves to play hard, defend vigorously, and contest the starters for loose balls. Mike Louis, Bob Larson, and Steve Hale rotated with the five starters as they were pressed and harassed by backups Larry Houchin, Jim Bailey, Jack Brown, and Mike Dershem. Only the coach's occasional whistle would give them time to catch their breath. As always, Sid encouraged them during the breaks. "We've come too far; now's not the time to rest!" His manner remained calm, but he was relentless in his demands for hustle. "Run! Press! Now get back and defend!" And as always, the players responded. It was clear that they respected their coach, but there was more to it than that. They truly admired him, and all of them shared his passion for playing the game right.

On Valentine's Day, 1967, the Braves of Tulsa Central arrived in Bartlesville with anything but love in their hearts. Outdoor temperatures were up, albeit briefly, and a warm, jam-packed gymnasium greeted them. From the opening tip, the outcome was never in doubt. On that evening in mid-February, the Braves were the victims of a coach's focus, a team's talent, and a rowdy crowd's enthusiasm. The proud Wildcats, from the top of the roster to the bottom, played their finest game of the season, defeating Central 82-49. In winning their twelfth consecutive game, the Cats ran their overall record to nineteen and one. The forty-nine points the defense surrendered was identical to their season average, best in the conference. Everyone on the team had a hand in the victory, with Scott Martin leading the scoring once again. The junior guard hit seven of eight field goal attempts, a big reason for the team's fifty-four percent shooting. He was joined in the shooting exhibition by Ernest (Moody) Guery with five for eight, Ernie (Eagle) Jackson with four for five, David Peterson with four for seven, and reserve Steve Hale with four for six. The leading trio from the bench (Hale, Louis, and Larson) combined for twenty points. Altogether, fourteen Wildcats saw action in the game, with twelve of them scoring. Their practice had paid off, and they were one game away from the tournament.

No better script could have been written for the conference finale, as the Friday game featured teams with identical league records of ten wins and one loss. The Ropers had lost to Bartlesville in overtime, and the Wildcats had been beaten by Ponca City. Each team ranked high statewide in both offense and defense, with only Oklahoma City Douglass looking better statistically. The stage was definitely set for a competitive climax to the regular season.

Thursday, February 16, brought a dramatic change in the weather. From a high of sixty-four on Wednesday, the mercury could only reach thirty-four degrees the next day. Biting north winds, virtually unimpeded in their flow from North Dakota, forced their way into Oklahoma overnight. All over Bartlesville, the residents awoke Friday morning to thermometers reading thirteen degrees—with the full force of high arctic winds blistering any exposed skin.

College High School Principal John Haley knew his decision would be unpopular. The school's field house, home of the basketball court, was also the venue for student pep rallies. There were no classrooms in the building, although the band and orchestra practiced there. The issue confronting Mr. Haley was the walk required to reach the field house from the classroom buildings. It would force hundreds of students to endure brutal winds and frigid temperatures, if only for the brief time to walk or run a couple of hundred feet. After careful consideration, his decision was "no pep rally." That announcement over the school's intercom system wouldn't have won the principal any popularity contests, but his wisdom is difficult to question. The students, including the players, spent the day in their classrooms, doubtlessly thinking of that evening's game. The afternoon high, which seemed almost tropical, reached thirty-five degrees.

A long day of school made even longer by the air of anticipation finally ended on Friday afternoon. Students and other Wildcat fans arrived early for a clash between the schools' "B" teams, also ranked at the top of the conference. By tipoff of the second game, the crowd was frenzied, making up for their missed opportunity to cheer earlier in the day. In physical appearance as well as statistically, the teams looked evenly matched. Rogers' backcourt pair of Jackie Richardson and Steve "Whipper" Montgomery was slightly smaller than Bartlesville's—their frontcourt combo averaged an inch taller. Both teams were ready!

The first half lived up to expectations and ended with the Wildcats leading by two, 23-21. The third quarter turned decisively toward the Ropers, though, with their shooting as hot as the Wildcats were cold. A surge of ten consecutive Rogers' points, aided by some poor Cats' passing, gave Rogers a 42-36 lead entering the fourth quarter. The Wildcats trimmed the margin to three points in the final two minutes, but Rogers ultimately prevailed with solid all-around performances, avenging their earlier loss, 59-54. The overflow crowd of over 2,000 left for home disappointed, but still proud of their second-place finish in a tough conference. Sid and the players, in contrast, immediately began thinking about their next game—just like they always did. Despite their focus, it's obvious from their writing over fifty years later that the players felt lasting remorse.

Boody's experience was both physically and emotionally difficult: "I recall the experience of a hip pointer in that game when we lost for only the second time all season. Their big guy, Steve Sizemore, was guarding Ernie in the lane. I thought I was gonna drive past him to the basket, but Sizemore slid over in an established position. I made an awkward jump towards him and the basket. He bent over and I jumped up over him with our backs touching. I fell straight to the floor on my hip and was called for the foul.

My hip felt like crap and both Wilber and Edgar (the two student managers) helped me off the court. That was a Friday night. The next morning at 7 a.m. I was to take the ACT exam at Central Pilgrim College. Was not my best effort in taking a test. I could hardly sit in an old wooden chair. And my feeling on that next Monday was probably the lowest I felt all year. We lost the conference, and I remember thinking we were still in position to play in the postseason, but that loss for me hurt as bad as the hip."

Pat Sears, 2020

CHAPTER 25

STILLWATER: ON THE REBOUND

Following the Wildcats' disappointing home loss to Tulsa Rogers, they and thirty-one other Class AAA teams had a week to prepare for their next games. Eight sites around the state readied their gyms for regional contests which would determine the state finalists. College High's team was assigned to the Stillwater regional, joining teams from Putnam City, Ponca City, and the host Stillwater Pioneers. Tipoff for the first game in all eight regions was scheduled for 7:00 p.m., Friday, February 24.

In Bartlesville, preparing for the regionals meant staying healthy, retaining focus, and emphasizing fundamentals. The Wildcats had enjoyed good health all season. Their only injuries were minor and short-lived—Eagle's ankle sprain in the second Edison game, and Petey's bruised shoulder from Jim Benien's body slam at Tulsa Central. Both recovered quickly and returned to top form in time for the playoffs.

Focus was never an issue for the team. Sid refused to let them think beyond the upcoming game, and overconfidence wasn't tolerated. One loss would end their season and they all knew it. Nearly three months into the season, the boys played as a unit. Around the state, other players, coaches, and media outlets recognized the unity displayed by the Wildcats. "Without their balance and selflessness, a team that small couldn't have possibly won nineteen games against that competition." That's how they were viewed by opposing coaches, and was reflective of Sid Burton's approach.

The Cats didn't use a zone defense, rather working daily on scrappy man-to-man drills, fighting through screens, and switching when necessary. Other teams were accustomed to gaining mismatches by weaves and setting screens. Gaining a mismatch against the Wildcats was next to impossible, as all five starters were nearly identical in size, and all were exceptional defenders. So practice that week involved working on defense, blocking out on rebounds, and hustling in transition. Up and down the court they ran, encouraged by Sid, and buoyed by their sense of knowing each other so well. And of course they shot. Known for their ability to make outside shots, they ran Sid's layup drills to perfection and took turns every day at the free throw line. They were a team, from starters through all seven reserves, who took nothing for granted.

At Thursday's practice, the last of the week, Sid backed off a little. He wanted the boys sharp but rested—ready to play but also healthy. Friday afternoon, the team, its coaches, and student managers climbed on the familiar "Yellow Dog" for the one hundred-mile, two-hour trip to Stillwater.

The town of Stillwater, which is roughly sixty miles from both Tulsa and Oklahoma City, is rich in basketball tradition. Slightly larger than Bartlesville, it is home to Oklahoma State University, a school with its own renowned basketball legacy. Named Oklahoma A&M until 1957, it produced back-to-back national championships in 1945 and '46. Names from those teams, like U.S. Olympic Coach Hank Iba and seven-footer Bob Kurland, were legends in Oklahoma and everywhere basketball was played.

The Wildcats' team bus arrived in Stillwater about ninety minutes prior to the game, with the team not thinking about creating another legend, but rather just winning the tournament's opening game. The players were loose and excited—this was what they lived for!

Marty Lowe recalls what happened after the Wildcats took the court for pregame drills:

"In the first round of the regionals held in Stillwater that year, College High was matched against Putnam City. The Pirates were from the Oklahoma City area and had not seen nor probably heard much about the Wildcats. As the teams were warming up before the tipoff, I noticed several of the PC players looking at the much smaller team on the opposite end of the court going through layup drills. A couple of them whispered to one another and nodded then proceeded to dunk the ball on their next trip through the layup line. They came back chuckling and looking down their noses at the Wildcats putting the ball off the glass in traditional layup style. Somebody on the Col-Hi team noticed what was going on (I know Steve Hale was aware of it since we have spoken about this event) because pretty soon Mike Louis (6'3") dunked, then Ernie Jackson (5'11") dunked, then 6'1" Steve Hale dunked with two hands, then 5'11" Pat Sears threw one down with authority, and so on it went. I had gone to the game with Pat's dad and we both had seen what was going on. We got a big kick out of the Putnam City team going from 'We'll show those pipsqueaks how to dunk a basketball' to 'Oh my God, did you see how high those guys can jump!' Their eyes were big as saucers—heck maybe even pie plates! Their attempt at intimidation backfired in a big way and they were more than a bit psyched out from that point. It was hilarious and quite memorable from a Wildcat fan perspective."

The Putnam City Pirates were indeed a much taller team than College High. Their backcourt players were a modest 5'9" and 6'2", but their front line players stood 6'3", 6'5", and 6'5", giving them a decisive height advantage. The Pirates' downfall, other than being shown up in pregame drills, might have been underestimating the strength and savvy of Moody and Eagle. Their jumping ability was clear before the game, but their way of storming the backboards became obvious soon after tipoff, as the two combined for nineteen rebounds. Overall, the Wildcats outrebounded the taller Pirates, 24-13, and outscored them, 66-53. Martin and Guery led the scoring with eighteen and sixteen points. Billy Hughes, later a good friend of Scott Martin's, was a reserve underclassman on the Pirates' bench who knew nothing about Bartlesville, but who watched in surprise as the shorter team methodically pulled away. Their win was easy compared to the Ponca City Wildcats'. The O-7's second Wildcat team edged past Stillwater in the night's second game, beating the host team, 44-42, in a defensive-minded overtime game. Putnam City and Stillwater, both very good teams, completed their seasons with 14-9 and 12-7 records, respectively. Both sets of Wildcats headed for home, looking forward to their third matchup of the season—the rubber game in which the losers would be eliminated.

Games in Stillwater on successive nights didn't allow much time to bask in their success. Fortunately for both of the winning teams, they knew each other well. There wasn't a lot to prepare for, and certainly no time to do it. It was cold that night in both Ponca City and Bartlesville, with temperatures near ten degrees. No player or coach on either team gave that a thought, though, as all minds were on getting some rest and being ready to play again on Saturday.

The teams had split their conference matchups, Ponca City narrowly winning in early January, 64-62, and then losing the rematch decisively, 79-55. Both teams had won on their home courts, so it was fitting that the final game for one of them would be contested on a neutral court. Sid had commented after the loss to Ponca City that "it would probably help." All his boys had done since then was win thirteen of fourteen games. It was time to see how much help it really was.

That time came around 3:00 Saturday afternoon as the aging yellow school bus left the College High parking lot once again. Passing west through town, it sluggishly accelerated to fifty miles per hour on U.S. Highway 60 and carried the team through the vast expanse of Osage County, home to many Native Americans of its namesake tribe. First west to Pawhuska, then south to Hominy, and an hour later across the Arkansas River near Cleveland with its surrounding oil fields, the bus safely arrived in Stillwater with a team ready to stretch their travel-worn legs and then take on their rivals. Led by their confident coach, they entered the site of Friday's victory, ready as always for a fun game of hoops.

Once again College High faced a much taller lineup. Ponca City still sported a pair of 6'4" front line players in Bobby Jack and Gerald Young. Like the Bartlesville players, they had gained valuable experience as the season played out, and had high hopes of leading their teammates to a big win.

The game was predictably hard fought, marred by early fouls called on key players. Both Young and Jack picked up three in the first period, and College High cashed in at the free throw line. By the final buzzer, six players had been disqualified—two from Bartlesville, plus Young, Jack, and two of their teammates. Meanwhile, Sid's players once again displayed exceptional balance, with Guery, Martin, Sears, and Peterson all scoring in double figures, and Moose Larson contributing solid defense coming off the bench. Ponca City kept it close most of the way, but ultimately fell for the second time in their three games, 67-57. Sid Burton's Wildcats, unlikely as it might have once seemed, were headed to the state quarterfinals in Tulsa.

CHAPTER 26

HOT TIME IN TULSA TOWN

The headliners for the 1967 State Championship tournament were unquestionably the Trojans from Oklahoma City Douglass. The throne was considered theirs, and all they had to do was show up and play. Of the remaining seven teams in the field, only Duncan, Norman, and Bartlesville's College High School teams were given a chance, and most predictions had them all playing for second place. That thinking was understandable, given the season-long dominance of Douglass. Besides, the teams rounding out the field lacked the resumes of the top four. Muskogee Central had lost twice to Bartlesville and finished fourth in the O-7 conference with a ten and ten record. They slipped through a relatively easy regional, knocking out Sapulpa and Shawnee, two teams with losing records. The reward for the Roughers? They would open the Fiftieth Annual Oklahoma High School Championships in the Tulsa Assembly Center against the Douglass Trojans.

Two Tulsa teams qualified for "state," but the Rogers Ropers weren't one of them. Magic Empire Conference teams from Memorial and McLain High Schools, both once lightly regarded, entered the tournament after surprising regional conquests. They had finished second and third in their league, but Memorial won its regional by routing conference champion Booker T. Washington, 71-59. Meanwhile, McLain's Scots pulled off another surprise by defeating Tulsa Rogers, 66-53, making a win over the O-7 champs look easy.

The biggest upset of the regionals' weekend was clearly the performance of the Generals of Oklahoma City U.S. Grant High School. Winners of only one game all season, and with eighteen losses, the Generals earned their way to Tulsa with narrow wins over Del City and Oklahoma City John Marshall. The tournament bracket paired them against powerhouse Norman, and College High would face Memorial.

Joining Douglass and Muskogee in the upper half of the bracket were McLain and highly regarded Duncan. Would-be prophets and self-styled experts could easily see a final foursome of Douglass, Duncan, Norman, and Bartlesville's College High School. Spoiler alert: It didn't happen that way.

The Wildcats, again with nearly a week between games, returned to practice with renewed confidence. They were entering a tournament with seven unfamiliar opponents, but they found themselves portrayed as "the team to beat"—except, of course, for OC Douglass. The problem with that logic for Sid and his crew was the performance of the U.S. Grant Generals. With only one win in their first nineteen games, they were living proof that anything could happen in a tournament. Like the previous weekend, the matchups in Tulsa meant "win or go home," and the Wildcats fully understood. Sid led their practices with quiet determination, still demanding hustle, but always tolerant of miscues. He projected confidence, but in a businesslike way. Sid was sure of himself, but not cocky, and that's how he expected his young men to play. So that's how they practiced: "pass and cut," "pass and screen," "press hard on defense," "keep the ball moving," and "PLEASE block out on rebounds!" Seldom did Sid raise his voice; never did he berate a player. Even in this, the most pressure-packed week of the season, he never lost his cool. Not surprisingly, that's how the players responded. If there was pressure, an observer at practice wouldn't notice it. The Wildcats were still just a bunch of guys who loved to play basketball, and that's what they did best.

February eased out during the week and March arrived, bringing a dramatic change in the weather. Bartlesville had experienced just one warm day in February—on the thirteenth when it reached seventy-two degrees. After low temperatures reached single digits during the regional action, Bartlesville recorded a high of eighty degrees on Wednesday, March 1. It climbed another degree on Thursday, the tournament's opening day, before settling back into the normal thirties, forties, and fifties for the weekend.

So with days getting longer and temperatures rising, Sid and his Wildcats boarded the bus late Thursday afternoon for the familiar trip to Tulsa. Tipoff was scheduled for 9:00 p.m., the final game of a critical day.

1967 Class AAA Boys

Oklahoma High School Championships

March 2-4, 1967 | Tulsa Assembly Center

State Tournament Bracket

The tournament opened at 2:00 p.m. Thursday, well before the "Yellow Dog" left College High. In front of a sparse crowd, the National Anthem was performed and the ball was tossed into the air between the first two contending teams. Norman, besides boasting a record of twenty-two and two, had a proud tradition in Oklahoma high school basketball. The Tigers' five state championships included wins over Muskogee in 1945, and Bartlesville in the 1955 and 1961 finals. More recently, they had been runners-up to Tulsa Webster in 1966. Norman was led by high-scoring big man Bob Campbell, with over twenty-four points per game, and the Tigers' twenty-two victories were most in the state.

The Tigers' opponents, the Generals from OC Grant, were terrible—and they knew it. Their plight was described by their head coach in the days leading up to the game.

"We're terrible, but here we are, going to State," admits U.S. Grant coach Don Metheny, whose Generals have the dubious distinction of tackling Norman's powerhouse in the opening round. When Grant received its trophy for winning the regional, one of Metheny's players asked, "Can we have our names put on it?" "Sure," Metheny replied. "Do you want your record put on it, too?"

Metheny admits he "was kinda mad when I saw we didn't draw Northwest (the heavy favorite) in the first game of the regional. We'd only won one game and I just wanted to get the season over with."

Bartlesville Examiner-Enterprise, March 1, 1967

Perhaps it was Metheny's cynicism, maybe some untold force, but it was more likely that Norman was simply worse that day than the Generals. In a game that left many attendees scratching their heads, the sloppily-played quarterfinal contest was lost by Norman, rather than won by Grant. The 40-39 loss sent the Tigers home deeply disappointed, and set the Generals up to play the winner of the College High-Memorial clash. At four and eighteen, they were on a roll!

Thursday's second game was scheduled to begin at 3:30. With kids leaving school, spring in the air, and a Tulsa team about to play, the 6,000-seat Tulsa Assembly Center began to fill up. It was still less than half full when McLain took the court to face the Duncan Demons. The Scots, with a front line averaging over 6'5", were confident as they watched the tournament's second smallest team warm up. Buoyed by their surprise win over Rogers, the McLain team knew they belonged in the race.

And a race it was! McLain kept the game close, holding Duncan to a 28-27 halftime lead, but a third quarter surge gave the Demons a seven-point edge entering the fourth quarter. The team that had traveled the furthest, about 190 miles, earned the right to spend the night in Tulsa, defeating McLain, 58-52.

The "Yellow Dog," carrying Sid Burton and his eager Wildcats, arrived at the Assembly Center just as the Douglass Trojans and Muskogee Roughers were tipping off. Fans from both cities were making their way to their seats, and the noise level was increasing. Both schools had avid followings, but the game wasn't determined by fan support. In fact, by midway through the third quarter, some Muskogee faithful were headed for home—disappointed but looking ahead to football season. Their 102-66 defeat didn't begin to reflect the dominance of Douglass. There was a reason why the Trojans were ranked number one throughout the season.

That left only the Wildcats' game versus Tulsa Memorial to determine the state's prestigious final four. The favorites, Douglass and Duncan, had prevailed in the upper half of the bracket, leaving the Cinderella Generals from U.S. Grant to face the winner of the 9:00 p.m. game between College High and Memorial. It was slightly after nine when the game tipped off, but neither team appeared affected by the late start. Memorial was, however, affected by the sheer talent of the Wildcats. After taking a two-point lead, the Chargers' hopes faded fast as Sid's patented up-tempo offense responded with thirteen consecutive points. That hot streak effectively ended Memorial's hopes of winning. Only a late surge with the game out of reach kept the score from being more lopsided than it was, with the Cats winning 62-49. Scott Martin dazzled the Bartlesville fans and others who stayed late by scoring twenty-two points and adding eight rebounds. The Wildcats, after some poor second quarter shooting, hit fourteen of twenty-eight field goal attempts in the second half, with Ernie Jackson scoring all ten of his points after the intermission. The tireless trio of Boody, Moody, and Eagle combined for sixteen more rebounds, giving the team a 29-25 edge over the taller Chargers. Boarding the bus for the trip home, they knew who their next opponents were, but they didn't know what to think of them. No one slept on the short ride back to Bartlesville.

The trip home was more exciting for some fans than for others. Marty Lowe describes his ride:

> "The town of Bartlesville supported the Wildcats quite well and since the state tournament was in Tulsa, a mere fifty miles away, there were lots of folks who made the drive to see the team play. Each night there were more cars than the previous night strung out along Highway 75. At that time, the road had been straightened out (it was called the 'beeline') but it was still a two-lane road. I got a ride to the tournament with classmate Larry 'Weasel' Lively, who was the photographer for the Examiner-Enterprise sports department at that time. After the opening quarterfinal game, he wanted to get back ASAP to develop the pictures he had taken and select the ones to be printed for the Friday evening paper. He was driving an old Ford van (official E-E vehicle) with a small six-cylinder engine. We were behind a long line of traffic that was driving at or slightly under the posted speed limit. Larry normally drove five to ten mph over the limit so he grew quite impatient.

At one point he could not stand it any longer, so he gave me his best 'watch this' look, pulled out into the oncoming traffic lane, and floored it. We passed at least twelve cars in that single move and certainly would have qualified for any driver safety film in the 'never do this' category. Larry was smiling from ear to ear and laughing the entire 'adventure' while I was yelling something like 'Weasel, you are going to get us killed!' We did get back to Bartlesville in time for the photos to make the Friday sports edition. The next morning at breakfast my mom remarked about the large number of folks who made the trip to see the game against Tulsa Memorial and the long lines of traffic from Bartlesville to Tulsa that were also on the return trip. Then shaking her head, she said 'When we were coming home there was some idiot in a van who passed about twenty cars and he was going about eighty! He must have been crazy.' I think I almost choked on my orange juice, and replied with something like 'Oh really?' then adroitly segued with 'How about that game last night?' to change the subject."

Friday's classes began way too early for a lot of College High students, including the basketball team. It had been close to midnight when the bus dropped them off in the parking lot. The players weren't overly tired, since Sid had been able to use his bench liberally. The notable exception was Pat Sears, who was battling a case of mononucleosis. "Sick as a dog," was how those close to Boody described him.

Mrs. Edith Hicks' journalism class frequently provided students a chance to conduct interviews over the school's intercom system during morning announcements. Conveniently, the effervescent Marty Lowe had recovered from his harrowing ride and embarrassing breakfast conversation, because Friday was his turn to show off his interview prowess with none other than Wildcat Coach Sid Burton.

"Principal John Haley introduced me with words like 'Take it away, Marty,' after which I replied 'thank you, Mr. Haley,' and launched into the interview with 'good morning, Sid.' When I got back to the room, Mrs. Hicks chewed me out in front of the class for calling a teacher by his given name, rather than Coach or Mr. Burton. I remember asking Sid if they got to play the taller and faster Oklahoma City Douglass team, whether they would play a 'slow down' game. He replied, 'No. We haven't played that style all year. We're going to play our game—up-tempo offense and tight defense.'"

Marty Lowe, 2020

For all the players, particularly Boody, the day of classes dragged on, seeming like it would never end. The final bell rang at last, releasing the energy of the team and its 1,500-plus backers into the warm spring air. Few had noted anything different in Sid's tone during his morning interview, but his response to Marty's question revealed that maybe—just maybe—the coach was for once looking beyond the next game. The student body could be forgiven for that. After all, the next opponent was the "pitiful but lucky" team from Oklahoma City Grant.

Fans from all over the basketball-crazy town loaded their sedans and station wagons for the trip to Tulsa's Assembly Center. Their beloved Phillips 66ers were in the home stretch of their season, but the upstart Wildcats had surged to the top as Bartlesville's favorite team. The high school had sent teams to the state semifinals before— in fact as recently as 1961. But high school basketball teams change dramatically from year to year, and the 1967 students and parents were a totally different group than the last time around. The excitement was genuine and contagious. The team evoked thoughts of "the little engine that could." The five starters, with only one standing as tall as 6', and their determined group of backups, had captured the heart of the town, exceeding everyone's expectations. Residents put aside differences in family background, personal wealth, religion, and race to unite behind everyone's special team. In the long, unending stream of southbound cars were rich and poor, Black and white, all united in support of the Wildcats.

The quarterfinal games of the tournament, played on Thursday, had been divided between two different sites. The Class AA games, featuring teams from slightly smaller schools, had been played at Oral Roberts University, site of the Wildcats' January tourney. The victors from those four games advanced to the AA semifinals, which were scheduled to alternate on Friday with the AAA games. The result was a 2:00 p.m. matchup between teams from Guthrie and Muskogee Manual, followed immediately by OC Douglass versus the Duncan Demons. The evening doubleheader was scheduled to tip off at 7:30 with Wewoka facing Oklahoma City Northeast, a team widely regarded as the second-best team in the state. In fact, an Oklahoma City group was reported to be seeking a site for the following weekend, where the champions of the two highest divisions, Douglass and Northeast, could compete for overall state honors.

So Bartlesville and OC Grant fans would have to wait until late evening, approximately 9:00 p.m., to see who would be doomed to play Douglass the following night. Douglass, that is, if they could continue their dominance by sending the Duncan Demons home. The Trojans accomplished their mission, right after Guthrie ended Manual's season. Duncan held Douglass far below their season scoring average, but thirty-four points and nineteen rebounds by the unstoppable Amos Thomas led to a comfortable 74-51 victory.

In the second AA semifinal, powerhouse OC Northeast required overtime to dispose of Wewoka, 64-62, keeping alive the hopes of a postseason showdown with local rival Douglass. The thrilling finish of the day's third game set the stage for the College High School Wildcats to face the underdog Generals of Oklahoma City Grant. Once again it was "win or go home."

Actually, it was "go home" for both teams, but the players and fans from Bartlesville went home as a far happier group. Whether it was luck or seldom seen skill that propelled the Generals to three straight postseason upsets, it all ran out on Friday night in Tulsa. The favored Wildcats displayed all the talent that got them there by running, passing, and shooting their way to an easy 64-45 win. Ernest Guery led the point parade with twenty points, followed by Scott Martin with twelve. Importantly, Sid was once again able to go to his bench early. All seven reserves saw action, and Moose Larson, despite missing all three of his field goal attempts, grabbed three big rebounds and played determined defense. After the game, Sid was asked about having to face Douglass the next day. Seemingly without emotion, he echoed his thoughts from the morning interview with Marty Lowe: "We're just going to have to play our game against them. We don't play a slow game very well, so we'll just have to try to run with them."

CHAPTER 27

DO YOU BELIEVE IN MIRACLES?

"Before I left my house for the bus the day of the game I went into my mom's bedroom and prayed. I said 'Lord, I know Douglass has a better team but I also know the best team doesn't always win. Help us play our best. Amen.'"

Scott Martin's private prayer reflected what most of the Wildcats were thinking—that indeed the Trojans of Oklahoma City Douglass were the better team. Their coach, Lawrence Cudjoe, was one of the greatest basketball minds in the state—if not the entire nation. The team Cudjoe assembled was also one of the nation's best. They were led by the state's best player, six-foot seven-inch center Amos Thomas, and had breezed through the season without being seriously challenged. Their scores against other Oklahoma City teams tell just how powerful the Trojans were, defeating OC Southeast 126-64, Capitol Hill 135-82, and Grant 104-56. Overall, they were averaging over eighty-three points per game, led by Thomas at nearly thirty points and fourteen rebounds per contest.

Douglass was far from a one-man show. In fact, if the Trojans had any weaknesses in the tournament, it was Coach Cudjoe having to trim his roster from their customary fourteen players to twelve. That might result in fewer substitutions than he was used to, or at least a different substitution pattern. No one offered Cudjoe any sympathy though. The eleven players surrounding Thomas were exceptional. All of them could have been starters for any other team in the state. Their shortest, listed anywhere between 5'7" and 5'11", was Josephus (Joe) Love. What Love might have lacked in height, he made up for with deadly outside shooting accuracy. Thomas and Love were joined in the starting lineup by 6'3" Mike Reese, 6'2" Nate Fowler, and 6'5" Hubert Greenwood.

Tipoff for the season's finale was scheduled for 9:00 p.m., or immediately following the Class AA game between OC Northeast and Guthrie. The bus ride to Tulsa on Saturday was identical to those on the two previous nights. Passing the Moose Lodge south of town, Moose Larson cleared his throat to get attention, and then led the team in their customary "Moose SA-LUTE!" The only difference that David Peterson noticed was that the southbound traffic was nearly bumper-to-bumper. With darkness falling, a look out the back window of the "Yellow Dog" revealed a string of headlights tailing the bus as far as Petey could see.

As the bus rolled into Tulsa for the third consecutive night and thirteenth time of the season, the players felt nerves they were unaccustomed to. For Pat Sears it was more than nerves. The "mono" which had plagued him all week was sucking the energy out of his body. At times he felt lifeless, questioning himself on how long he could play—how much he could contribute. But Boody was like everyone else on that Wildcat bus. They had come too far, worked too hard, and had such a love for the game and each other that he wouldn't be left out of his final high school game. Some of the others felt discomfort too, perhaps from an understandable case of "butterflies" in their stomachs.

Boody had visited his family physician the day prior to the game. Dr. Owen wasn't just his doctor—he was a friend. Boody and James

Owen, third of the doctor's four sons, had been close buddies for years. They had played together in a nearby creek since elementary school. Dr. Owen knew of his patient's passion for basketball, but Boody could read his mind. "He knew playing wasn't in my best interest, but he didn't tell me not to. That's all I needed," he recalled.

The bus pulled into its assigned space in the Assembly Center parking lot about halfway through the Class AA game. Sid led the team down the now-familiar hallway to the locker room, where they quickly donned their dark game shorts and jerseys.

Everyone on the Wildcats' roster remembers the pre-game warmups. No one sitting in the stands that night needs Scott Martin's description to recall the feeling as the players were introduced.

> *"When they came out to warm up, the first three guys dunked it. After they announced their starters and size, they announced us—four guys 5'11" and one guy 6'—the crowd was laughing."*

Finally, three months and two days after their opening game versus Miami, the Wildcats' season finale was underway. The largest crowd to see them all season, estimated at more than 6,000 fans, was in a frenzy. There was a vivid contrast in the appearance of the teams—one obviously much taller than the other—but their style of play was strikingly similar: fast breaks, pound the backboards, and press aggressively on defense. Wear the other team out! Sid Burton and Lawrence Cudjoe shared the same philosophy of basketball. Keep the tempo up and force the opponent into making mistakes.

Sid had been advised by other coaches that the only chance his team had against Douglass was to slow the game down. "Keep the score in the fifties and you might have a chance." The underdog coach would have none of that! He had confidence in his players' ability to handle the ball, to play rugged defense, and hopefully show their superior conditioning. Boody's durability was questionable at best, but Sid was unaware of how sick he was.

No one could have been disappointed by the first quarter. With both teams employing a full-court press, the ball handling of Scott Martin and Joe Love dazzled the crowd. The fans loved good basketball, and the Cats and Trojans gave it to them. Back and forth the teams went, Douglass controlling the backboards, but the Wildcats failing to back down. The tone was set in the first two minutes, with the teams swapping the lead four times. The taller team displayed confidence—the smaller team showed grit. The first quarter, in which neither team could stretch a lead, ended with the Trojans up 18-15.

At that point, Coach Sid Burton employed a bit of a surprise. Douglass had a thorough scouting report on the Wildcats, but it appeared that they weren't ready for Sid's move—to insert the six-foot, three-inch senior, Mike Louis, into the game at an early stage. Louie, simply stated, was outstanding throughout the second period. During one stretch, he and his teammates combined for eleven consecutive points, as part of a stunning run of eleven straight made baskets.

Martin drives between Joe Love and Amos Thomas

Then, with his height partially offsetting the Trojans' advantage, Louie's twelve points carried the Cats to a 46-43 halftime lead. Douglass was clearly caught off-guard by the early addition of Louis, and Amos Thomas got into early foul trouble.

The Wildcats' locker room was subdued at halftime. Sid's demeanor was the same as it always was. Quiet, yet confident, he implored his followers to continue doing what they do best. If anything special was learned from the first half, it was that Douglass might be tiring a bit. That was all the more reason to keep pressing on defense and forcing the ball ahead quickly on offense. No one, not even Douglass, exceeded College High's ability to handle the ball. The players realized how hard it was to stop the Trojans from scoring, but they also knew Douglass was having a hard time stopping them. Petey remembers Assistant Coach Don Calvert telling the players, "Be patient—those long shots they're making will turn into long rebounds. Keep your position and be heads-up!"

A confident Wildcat team jogged back onto the court for a brief shoot-around before the game resumed. It appeared that no one had left their seats, and the crowd greeted both teams with enthusiasm. Two differences from the pre-game drills—the Trojans weren't smiling and their fans weren't laughing. The second half would be all business.

The third quarter resembled the first, with the teams continuing their fast-paced play, and the Wildcats pressing the length of the court. Fouls continued to mount, causing frequent trips to the free throw line by both teams. The Cats remained composed, protecting the ball well and moving it crisply. The pace looked like it favored the underdogs, but they couldn't find a way to extend the lead. In fact, Douglass jumped ahead briefly, 54-53, halfway through the period. That was short-lived though, as Martin converted a free throw for a three-point play, and Peterson added two free throws. The lead back in their favor, the Wildcats held on to remain ahead, 60-59, at the end of the third quarter. The close, back and forth play of the first three quarters set the stage for a nail-biter that virtually no one had expected.

None of the former Wildcat players has ever mentioned being tired during the game. However, Scott Martin, who was usually matched up against Joe Love, recalls the Douglass point guard facing him and saying to no one in particular, "I'm so tired; I'm so tired."

A one-point game, the state championship at stake, a packed gymnasium, and an overwhelming favorite battling to conclude an undefeated season—Hollywood couldn't have produced a better script. The Douglass and College High cheerleaders led their boisterous fans through the school cheers for the last time of the season. A loosely organized group of Bartlesville boys calling themselves "the Wildroots" had cheers of their own, which they used in response to the loud, rhythmic yells from the Douglass fans.

"California oranges, Arizona cactus—we play your team just for practice." That prompted a Douglass reply, which was countered by "Red Rover, Red Rover, send your cheerleaders over." Just like the teams on the court, back and forth they went, at one time the Wildroots yelling "We can't hear you."

Amidst the clamor and growing suspense, the teams took the court for the final eight minutes of the season. The Wildcats' hopes rose almost immediately as the 6'7" Amos Thomas picked up his fifth foul and took a seat on the bench. The Trojans bounced back with six consecutive points, however, and took a 65-60 lead with the clock reading 6:52. Before it reached 4:02, the teams had traded two more baskets, but a Douglass free throw stretched the Trojans' lead to six, at 70-64. Sid Burton, his team in a deepening hole, called timeout. He and his assistant, Don Calvert, remained calm even as the crowd grew increasingly boisterous. According to Petey, Coach Calvert assured them that they would score enough points to win. All they had to do was "play great defense and keep Douglass from scoring." Sid, knowing how important those words were, dug deep for a way to help make it possible. Turning to Moose Larson, Sid said, "Get in there and make something happen."

From the sideline huddle, the team broke onto the court, executed a play to get Moody Guery open, and closed the lead to four points. Unfortunately for the Cats, the 6'2" Nat Fowler answered with a basket and the lead was back to six points with 3:26 on the clock. Douglass 72—College High 66. At that point, Sid and his boys needed more than great defense; they needed a miracle.

Call it a miracle, call it magic, or maybe call it experience from those many years of playing together. From the days of their Boys Club championship team to the evenings when some had played for the Phillips 33ers, the five Wildcats on the floor trusted each other and refused to panic. The tireless, superbly conditioned Guery then found himself open for a short jump shot at the 2:29 mark. The Trojans continued to tire and slowed the pace a bit. Then, Moose Larson, inserted for his defense, stole the ball with 1:28 remaining. Scott Martin quickly hit a jumper of his own, set up the full-court press, and immediately took a charging foul from Joe Love. Momentum appeared to favor the underdog Cats, but a minute remained and they were still trailing by two.

That didn't last long as Petey drove down the lane, drew the defender, then dished the ball to Moody for the tying bucket. With less than a minute to play, it was the Trojans playing with desperation. Rather than hold the ball for a last-second shot, they worked the ball inside to the usually dependable Lee Gaines, who missed his first attempt, grabbed his own rebound, and missed again from point-blank range. Battling underneath like the seasoned warrior he was, David Peterson rebounded the miss and immediately signaled for a timeout. Douglass had mysteriously allowed the Wildcats one more chance.

With thirteen seconds left in regulation play, and the score tied at seventy-two, Sid drew up a play. Surprisingly, he elected to keep Moose Larson in the game. Sid had only used three reserves (Moose, Steve

Hale, and Mike Louis) in the three-game tournament, and Moose had taken only four shots, missing them all. With Amos Thomas and two other Trojan starters disqualified with five fouls, Sid chose Larson over the taller Louis "on a hunch." Moose was rugged, a good rebounder, and a smart team player. He would be okay.

Sid's strategy was to have Petey inbound the ball to point guard Scott Martin, who would hold the ball long enough to get the other four players in motion, and then either shoot or get it to Guery for the final shot. Petey was the third option. Jackson and Larson would screen if needed to spring someone free, and then crash the board for a rebound.

Both teams broke from their huddles and the referee handed Petey the ball and whistled for action to resume. With the ball in play and the clock ticking past the ten-second mark, all went as planned, except that both Martin and Moody were double-teamed. Douglass Coach Cudjoe had accurately anticipated who would be the main Wildcat weapons. Martin briefly considered passing into the post to Jackson with Eagle kicking it back out to him but was not sure of getting the ball back in time for a clean shot. Looking quickly to his left, Scott found the unguarded Moose Larson near the baseline, about fifteen feet from the basket and fed him the ball. Surprised but unfazed, there was nothing Moose thought he could do but shoot. With that, Martin's hopes of getting the ball back were abruptly dashed. Deaf to the roar of the crowd, shoot he did! Moose guided the ball up, and with 6,000 people holding their breath, down it came —nothing but net—and a hero was born!

With three seconds remaining, Douglass inbounded the ball and missed a futile attempt to tie the game. The College High School Wildcats were state champions for the first time in the school's history and it was all over but the shouting.

Scott Martin: "My prayers were answered!"

CHAPTER 28

Bedlam Reigns

The last-second shot by Lee Gaines had just caromed off the rim, not even reaching the floor, when the avalanche of Wildcat fans poured out of the stands. The leading edge of the onslaught reached Moose Larson first, and he was buried by teammates and fellow students before being lifted onto their shoulders. The explosion of pent-up emotion that followed the buzzer was deafening. The scene can be described in many ways, but chaos and bedlam are words that are frequently used. Delirious Wildcat fans covered the Assembly Center court from one basket to the other, and from sideline to sideline. Other players, like Scott Martin, joined Moose for the triumphant ride to nowhere. Just being on someone's shoulders was that moment's version of Cloud Nine. The exuberance of triumph couldn't be tempered by the squelched feeling of disbelief. No one—absolutely no one—saw this coming!

Sid, meanwhile, graciously shook hands with the disappointed Lawrence Cudjoe and headed straight for the locker room. There, ready to celebrate with his players, he found the place empty. He returned to the door and then, for the first time, became aware of the din outside. Upon reaching the court, he too was mobbed by elated students. "We won! We won! We just beat Douglass! Can you believe what just happened?" Over and over the shouts were heard. Then a small group chanting "We're Number One" turned into a larger group bellowing it out. The College High School Wildcats were actually Number One. Bedlam reigned, and the instant, unlikely hero was Moose Larson. He had just completed the state tournament with one for five shooting and no one remembered the first four shots. He made the one that counted.

Martin, Larson, and Peterson riding high

As the celebration continued, the noise subsided enough for strained conversations to take place. Several reporters finally located Sid. "We dazzled them with our height," he joked. "We're just a different kind of team than anyone they faced all year. I don't think they knew how to handle us. On the other hand," he continued, "we're at our best when things get wild and wooly. I can't say enough about how the boys reacted to the pressure."

When asked about Larson's final shot, Sid wasn't concerned. "I hate to see a boy pass up an open shot," he said. Moose took it all in stride. "I didn't want to shoot, but I thought if I didn't that we probably wouldn't get another shot." With that, he drifted away into the crowd as the coach and players gathered for the trophy presentation.

The game's box score only tells a small part of the story.

Bartlesville College High

	FG	FT	REB	PF	TP
Guery	8-14	4-6	9	4	20
Peterson	2-6	3-3	4	3	7
Jackson	2-6	3-4	5	4	7
Martin	7-17	6-6	3	1	20
Sears	2-8	0-0	4	2	4
Louis	5-9	4-7	2	2	14
Hale	0-0	0-0	1	1	0
Larson	1-1	0-0	1	0	2
Total	**27-61**	**20-26**	**29**	**17**	**74**

Oklahoma City Douglass

	FG	FT	REB	PF	TP
Greewood	1-3	2-2	9	5	4
Reese	3-3	0-1	5	5	6
Thomas	9-16	4-5	10	5	22
Fowler	8-13	1-4	11	0	17
Love	6-12	0-0	0	2	12
Gaines	2-13	4-4	3	1	8
Rich	1-5	1-4	1	3	3
Harris	0-0	0-0	1	0	0
Total	**30-65**	**12-20**	**40**	**21**	**72**

HALFTIME: **Bartlesville 46, Douglass 43**

As expected, the Wildcats were outrebounded by the taller Trojans. It was the first time all season that the Cats lost the battle of the boards. Field goal percentages were extremely close—44.3% for College High, 46.2% for Douglass. Notably, Amos Thomas was held to twenty-two points, well below his season average of thirty. Ernie Jackson, as always, led the defensive effort, but was helped a lot by his swarming, aggressive teammates.

Not surprisingly, Scott Martin and Ernest Guery led the Cats in scoring. Their combined fifteen for thirty-one field goal shooting, plus ten for twelve from the charity stripe, led to their being named to the *Tulsa World's* all-tournament team. They were joined on the Class AAA first team by the Trojans' Amos Thomas and Mike Reese, and Jerry Hopkins of Oklahoma City Grant. Ernie Jackson was selected for the second team.

Other numbers that stood out: Petey's perfect free-throw shooting, which contributed to the team's seventy-seven percent, the one statistic that heavily favored the Wildcats; the fourteen points by Louie off the bench, twelve of them in the big second quarter; and finally, the perfect field goal shooting of Moose—yes, the same Moose who hadn't made a shot in the tournament.

More accolades would come, but the team had more celebrating to do. Following their showers and change of clothes, they boarded the "Yellow Dog" and headed for one of Tulsa's newest "places to be"—the Camelot Inn. Located at Interstate 44 and Peoria Avenue, the Camelot had opened in 1965 and hosted such celebrities as Elvis Presley and Vice President Richard Nixon. It was there, in the luxurious lobby, that Boody Sears finally collapsed. His mono caught up with him and he plopped into an oversized chair as his teammates filed past, accepting the invitation of Mr. Bill Martin and the Bartlesville Quarterback Club to enjoy a late-night steak dinner.

———

Oklahomans awoke Sunday morning to news many hadn't heard before going to bed. The *Daily Oklahoman* in the state capital expressed shock that its city's Douglass Trojans had been upset by the unlikeliest of foes, the College High Wildcats of Bartlesville. Their woes were partially offset by the Class AA results, with Oklahoma City Northeast taking home the trophy. Bartlesville's *Examiner-Enterprise* featured a banner headline in its sports section which read: Wildcats are Number 1! And finally, the *Tulsa Sunday World* greeted its morning readers with a page-wide sports section headline reading: WILDCATS STUN DOUGLASS FOR CROWN. Both the Tulsa and Bartlesville papers included sub-headlines mentioning Bob Larson's last-second shot in the 74-72 victory.

Most of the Wildcat team, appropriately, slept well past the delivery of the morning papers. The notable exception was the always dependable Petey, who was up before dawn, peddling his bicycle as always, to get the news out. There was no Saturday edition, so residents catching up on sports news found reports of the Cats' wins over both Grant and Douglass. By the time the town's newest basketball heroes awoke, the entire town was abuzz with excitement it had seldom seen. Rich and poor, Blacks and whites, all shared a bond in basketball. And this team, unlike the popular Phillips 66ers, was truly representative of the entire community. The players were raised in different neighborhoods and attended different elementary and junior high schools. Most of them started when schools were still segregated. Some were trained as youngsters on the Phillips court—others at the Boys Club. Just as the coach and players loved each other, the people of Bartlesville had fallen in love with Sid and his boys. They had just pulled off the greatest upset in Oklahoma high school sports history, and they had represented their community with determination, class, and diversity.

> *The town of Bartlesville was elated over the state championship victory. The Board of Education declared the next school day, March 6, as Wildcat Day in celebration of the victory. The entire student body of Sooner High School, which only had a sophomore and junior class, was bused to College High School for the celebration. The victory was the talk of Bartlesville for a long time.*

Monday arrived with a new kind of school day at College High. The celebration began in the gym, site of so many of the Wildcats' thrilling victories, at 8:00 a.m. For the next two hours there were speeches, skits, songs, cheers, and general frivolity. Nothing raised the noise level like the introduction of Sid and the players. The basketball team wasn't the only reason to celebrate that morning, for over the weekend the boys' swimming team had won its sixth consecutive state title, and the girls' team had won for the second straight year. Through no fault of their own, other than being so good, those championships didn't generate as much excitement, largely because their excellence was taken for granted.

That wasn't true of the hoopsters. They were crazy good, and no one in the state knew it until Saturday night. Sure, they were ranked second in the most recent polls, but everyone knew that Douglass was head and shoulders better than anyone else in the state. That is, everyone knew except Sid and his boys. They watched as the cheering continued, with the noise in the jam-packed gym reaching levels seldom recorded, even in tight basketball games. One of the highlights was a skit featuring Larry Lively as Moose Larson—yes, the same "Weasel" who had driven eighty miles per hour from Tulsa four days earlier. Weasel took a ball onto the court and stood in the same relative spot Moose Larson had used for his history-making shot. Try as he might, Weasel failed in ten consecutive attempts to replicate the winning basket. Ten straight misses! With the crowd chanting, "We want Moose, we want Moose," Bob Larson finally stepped onto the court and took a ball to the same spot—just to show the crowd how it was done. The problem? Five straight misses, and with the crowd in hysterics, Moose sheepishly found a place to sit down.

It was all over too soon, but the message Principal John Haley delivered at the conclusion was music to the students' ears. There would be no classes the rest of the day, and the revelers were invited back for the victory "sock hop" at 7:30 that evening. With that, another boisterous cheer went up, and the students and teachers slowly but happily cleared the gym.

In the days that followed, as Petey described, the Wildcats were the talk and the toast of the town. The All-State Boys Basketball Team was announced, headlined by Amos Thomas and Oklahoma City Northeast's Ray Russell. Spurred by his leadership on the Wildcats' championship drive, Ernest Guery was a natural selection for the star-studded roster. Voters were barred from voting for juniors, keeping the otherwise shoo-in, Scott Martin, off the list for another year. Following that announcement, to the surprise of no one, Coach Sid Burton was named Oklahoma's "Coach of the Year" by the *Tulsa World*. Terrell Lester, a sports writer for the paper summed it up:

> *Sid Burton is the epitome of tranquility. Not even a state championship in his second full season of coaching can change his image. For bagging the biggest prize with the smallest ammunition in the shortest length of time, the amiable Bartlesville College High coach has been selected Coach of the Year.*

An unfortunate but significant footnote to the season was the exclusion of Ernest (Moody) Guery from a notable postseason event. The "Faith 7 Bowl" is an annual basketball contest featuring the ten best high school players from Texas and Oklahoma. Sid was contacted after the competing players were announced, and was told by the Oklahoma coach that Moody would have been selected, except the coach had "met his quota." In that conversation, the state of high school basketball in Oklahoma was sadly but accurately revealed.

ODE TO THE COACH

There was never a doubt about how to start out
when writing a book about Sid.
It begins with his wife, the love of his life,
and the great times he had as a kid.

He and Jan were glad through good times and bad
for the love of family and friends.
Their faith ever strong would lead them along
with a spirit that still never ends.

He served his nation with dedication,
then earned a second degree.
With grad school behind him, fate would soon find him
back home teaching history.

With wisdom and prudence, he guided his students,
making history fun for them all.
And when the bell rang he'd assemble the gang
of boys who liked playing ball.

What he loved in sport, whether diamond or court,
was regardless of who won or lost,
That the lessons in life learned from friendly strife
were always worth more than they cost.

But once came a year in his worthy career
when he led an exceptional team.
Saying size doesn't matter, they scaled a steep ladder,
pursuing a magical dream.

With Eagle and Boody, and Petey and Moody,
and a junior named Martin thrown in,
Sid took his boys and showed them the joys
that only occur when you win.

But even with Sport they needed support,
and Sid found it in Louie and Moose.
Though smaller by far, and facing a star,
he managed to keep the team loose.

As they had from the start, the bench did their part,
and they'll always remember the joys
Of a game beyond reason and a magical season
as part of Sid and the Boys.

EPILOGUE

Following the championship season, half of the players graduated from College High School. They included Ernest Guery, Ernie Jackson, Bob Larson, Mike Louis, David Peterson, and Pat Sears. The remaining student-athletes were divided, with Steve Hale and Jack Brown transferring to the east side's Sooner High School. Of the starting five, only Scott Martin remained at College High School, where he was joined on the following year's team by Mike Dershem, Larry Houchin, Jim Bailey, and manager-turned-player, Don Wilber.

All of the players enjoyed noteworthy experiences following that memorable season. Ernie Jackson received a scholarship to attend the University of Notre Dame, where he played football for two seasons before a knee injury ended his career. He graduated with honors, was a Rhodes Scholar finalist, and earned an academic postgraduate scholarship. He later graduated from Columbia

Bettye and Ernie Jackson

University Law School and became a successful government lawyer. He resides today, as he has for many years, in Washington, DC, with his wife, Sally Ethelston, and their godson.

Pat Sears played junior college basketball and baseball (lettering in the latter) for Northern Oklahoma College before interrupting his education to serve in the U.S. Army. Upon being discharged, he enrolled in the University of Oklahoma, where he earned a degree in marketing in 1976. His career began as a YMCA director in Tulsa, and was followed by years in insurance, computers, and electronics. He and his wife Diane continue to call Tulsa, the site of his greatest sports experience, their home. Over the years, they have shared their home with numerous foreign exchange students.

Like his friend Boody, Ernest (Moody) Guery opted for junior college basketball, attending Independence (Kansas) Community Junior College. He also left school for military service, returning later to Panhandle State College, where he earned his degree. Ernest later worked in the aerospace industry in California before succumbing to cancer in 2004. He left behind a wife, Estella, and five children.

David Peterson returned to Stillwater, site of some of his best high school memories, and enrolled in Oklahoma State University. He played on the freshman basketball and varsity tennis teams. Another player on the freshman basketball team was former Oklahoma City Douglass star, Amos Thomas. Upon first meeting his state final rival, Thomas told Petey that his explanation to Oklahoma City fans when asked about the game, was that "those little guys just flat outplayed us." Petey also faced off against former Wildcat tennis and basketball teammate, Scott Martin, in a Big Eight tennis tournament. David earned two degrees from Oklahoma State, including an MBA, and enjoyed a long career in the oil and gas processing business. He joined Cities Service in Tulsa, experienced several organizational changes, and moved with the company to The Woodlands, Texas. He continues to live there with his wife of nearly fifty years, former College High cheerleader Linda Markee.

Petersons joined by the Burton family

Petey recalls: "My senior year at OSU, I played at the number three position on the OSU varsity tennis team. At the end of the season I reached the semifinals of the Big Eight tennis tournament on Friday, May 21, in Stillwater. The finals of the tournament were to be held on Saturday, May 22. That was also the day that I was to be married in Bartlesville. Once I saw who I would need to beat to reach the finals, I knew my wedding plans would not need to be changed. My semifinal opponent was OU's Scott Martin. Scott had no problem beating me quickly enough that I was only ten minutes late for my rehearsal dinner in Bartlesville on Friday night."

Following the memorable championship year, Scott Martin's career as a Wildcat continued through the spring of 1968. In his senior year he was named an All-State quarterback in football and was again a state champion tennis player. He received a scholarship to play basketball and tennis, just as his father had, at the University of Oklahoma. Scott excelled in both sports, winning conference tennis tournaments and receiving the 1972 Naismith Award as the nation's best basketball player under six feet tall. That year he was also invited to participate in the Olympic Trials, and was selected for the All-Big Eight Academic basketball team. Upon leaving OU, he ranked seventh on the team's all-time scoring list. Scott was awarded an NCAA postgraduate scholarship and earned his MBA at Tulsa University. By age thirty, he was one of the youngest bank presidents in Tulsa's history. He and his wife Carole are happily retired in Tulsa.

The starters weren't the only players to achieve success in later life. Mike Louis received a basketball scholarship, Jim Bailey and student manager Don Wilber graduated from medical schools and became noted Oklahoma physicians, Bob Larson graduated from Furman University, as did Jack Brown from Kansas State University. Larry Houchin graduated from the University of Oklahoma and was a successful Tulsa businessman for many years. Steve Hale attended Northeastern Oklahoma State in Tahlequah, and later earned a teaching degree from Oklahoma Wesleyan in Bartlesville.

Finally, the beloved coach Sid Burton, true to his heartfelt decision that he could coach no longer in Bartlesville, moved with his family to Norman, where he earned his PhD from the University of Oklahoma. He followed that by resuming his coaching career, first at Del City High School and then at Rose State College in Midwest City, Oklahoma. He was inducted into the Bartlesville Sports Hall of Fame in 2019. Sid resides, as he has for many years, in Norman. He continues to enjoy the love and respect of "the boys."

Sid and the Boys, 2019

Kneeling: Marty Lowe

Standing: David Peterson, Ernie Jackson, Scott Martin, and Pat Sears

IN MEMORIAM

Jo Allyn Lowe
(1914-1975)
First Executive Director
Bartlesville Boys Club

Ernest Guery
(1949-2004)
College High School Wildcat
1967 All-Tournament and All-State selectee

Larry Houchin
(1949-2011)
College High School Wildcat
President, Southern Hills Country Club, Tulsa

Don Calvert
(1937-2020)
Assistant Varsity Basketball Coach
1966-67 College High School Wildcats

ACKNOWLEDGEMENTS

Writing this book was a true labor of love, enabled by the full cooperation of Coach Sid Burton and the men who played for him in 1966 and
1967. In particular, the four surviving starters on that team—Ernie
Jackson, Scott Martin, David Peterson, and Pat Sears—have been
with me from start to finish. I first met with Sears and Marty Lowe
in February 2020. Marty and Boody were high school classmates and
lifelong friends, and I've known both of them since we were teenagers.
Boody accompanied me on a fourteen-hour roundtrip to Ames, Iowa,
to visit our friend and former Phillips 66ers player and coach, Gary
Thompson. A month later, Boody, Marty, and I were joined at Sid's
house in Norman by David Peterson, who drove from The Woodlands,
Texas, for a nearly six-hour visit with Sid and his son Butch.

On those two trips from my home in Charlotte to Oklahoma City,
thankfully before the COVID-19 pandemic restricted my travel, I also
met in person with Sue Freiberger, Dr. Don Wilber, Sue Reynolds, Bill
Dutcher, and Jim Hess—all graduates of College High School in the
sixties. On the first trip, thanks to considerable contributions from Sue
Freiberger, Don, Pat, and Scott Martin, I needed a new, large suitcase to
carry home scrapbooks, yearbooks, and other memorabilia that have
helped me immensely. On that same trip, I met with Bartlesville Sports
Hall of Fame president Bob Pomeroy, and former 66ers All-American
Charlie Bowerman. All of those interviews were exceedingly helpful,
as well as very enjoyable.

When I encountered a lengthy delay in my return flight from Oklahoma City, I was able to meet Coach Kendal Cudjoe in the gymnasium at Classen SAS High School. Kendal, who, like his father, once coached at Oklahoma City Douglass, recounted watching the 1967 championship game in person as a seven-year-old boy.

Following my second trip to Oklahoma, while largely restricted by the pandemic to my home, I relied heavily on phone conversations, texts, and emails. Since March, I have had hundreds of communications with the four starters, and dozens with others, including Sid, Gary Thompson, and Jim Hess. For reinforcement of some details regarding the basketball season, I often turned to newspaper reports from the *Bartlesville Examiner-Enterprise*, the *Tulsa Daily World*, and the defunct *Tulsa Tribune*. While I didn't use their material directly (except where cited), I'm grateful that all three newspapers provided essential background information. I'm appreciative of time spent on the phone with Mike Tupa, sports editor of the *Examiner-Enterprise*, and Berry Tramel, columnist for *The Oklahoman*. I also appreciate the cooperation of the Bartlesville Area History Museum, and particularly its collections manager, Debbie Neece. A local artist, Carolyn Mock, approved the use of her painting of the area west of Bartlesville inside the back cover.

No one, aside from the team, provided more help than Marty Lowe and Dr. Don Wilber. Marty played football with Sears, Jackson, Martin, and others prior to the basketball season, and Don served as the student manager that season before joining the varsity team the following year. I would be remiss in not saying that Marty's father, Jo Allyn Lowe, and Don's father, Roy Wilber, were inspirations to me in my formative years in Bartlesville. Like Scott Martin and a number of reserves, Don graduated in 1968. Don's nephew, Landon Morgan, provided a great assist by formatting the maps that appear in the book.

I appreciate the enlightening phone conversations I had with Bob (Moose) Larson, Mike (Louie) Louis, and "Big Jack" Brown, as well as Cecil Epperly, who followed Sid Burton as the College High basketball coach. Mike June, College High School Class of 1963, was always there to help with the research.

The outstanding book by Louise S. Robbins, *The Dismissal of Miss Ruth Brown: Civil Rights, Censorship, and the American Library*, provided valuable background information, particularly for Chapter 8.*

Special thanks go to several professionals in their fields: Cristina Smith for monthly counseling in the art of getting a book written and published; Valerie Costa for editing; and Christy Collins and Constellation Book Services for cover, layout design, and much more. Thanks also to the volunteers who read this book and contributed mightily to the finished product. They, alphabetically, are Kay Baughman, Kay Earhart, Marty Lowe, Connie Wirth, and Garry Zopf. All of them did much more than read and comment. They provided continual encouragement and support throughout the process.

Above all, I'm grateful to my family. I received daily support—including brainstorming, editing, encouragement, and more—from my wife, Jan, and a steady stream of ideas, feedback, editing, and website support from our daughters—Kristy, Melanie, Amanda, and Kara. Melanie, a professional writer, provided the bulk of the manuscript's editing. They are exceptionally talented and supportive, and I love all of them. Our older son, Casey, provided long distance support, and our nine-year-old son, Scott, did his best to put up with a very busy dad. Our then-eight-year-old grandson Jake Barber developed the concept for the cover art. As I wrote in the beginning, this was a labor of love.

My one regret is that my late brother, Lieutenant Colonel Patrick William McCullough, didn't live to enjoy this project. Pat graduated from College High School in 1967, played football with Martin, Lowe, Jackson, Sears, Larson, and Brown, and was a track teammate of Sears, Lowe, and Jackson. He graduated from the Air Force Academy in 1971, was a decorated Vietnam War pilot, and served his country for decades. We laid Pat to rest in Arlington National Cemetery in 2019, a year after his death.

---

* University of Oklahoma Press, 1950

"West of the City" by Carolyn Mock

PHOTO CREDITS

Cover	Basketball team, courtesy of "Col Hi," 1967 College High yearbook
Frank Phillips	Bartlesville Area History Museum
Phillips Mansion	Mike McCullough
The Mound	Bartlesville Area History Museum
Price Tower	Bartlesville Area History Museum
Skyline	Bartlesville Area History Museum
Houses	Bartlesville Area History Museum
Westside community	Bartlesville Area History Museum
Douglass School	Bartlesville Area History Museum
AAU Champs	Marty Lowe, Bartlesville Boys Club
Maps	Bartlesville Area History Museum, enhanced by Landon Morgan
Boys Club fishing	Marty Lowe, Bartlesville Boys Club
College High School	Bartlesville Area History Museum
Field House	Bartlesville Area History Museum
Phillips 66ers	Bartlesville Examiner-Enterprise
The Letter	Original by Pat (Boody) Sears, reproduced by Carl McCullough
Boots Adams' office	Bartlesville Area History Museum
Holbrook, Burton, and Stidham	Bartlesville Area History Museum
Kendal Cudjoe	Carl McCullough
McLain tourney	Bartlesville Examiner-Enterprise
Martin's layup	Winston's Studio, Bartlesville, OK
Championship celebration	Winston's Studio, Bartlesville, OK
Bettye and Ernie Jackson	Ernie Jackson
Petersons and Burtons	David Peterson
Sid and the Boys	Marty Lowe
"West of the City"	Painting by Carolyn Mock

For accompanying musical suggestions and to download
discussion and study guides, visit www.SidAndTheBoys.com

Made in the USA
Coppell, TX
21 May 2021

55973571R00115